CONSIDER IT DONE...

Miracles for a Wounded Soldier

☆ ☆ ☆

John Pirinelli
Risë Pirinelli
Ruth Pirinelli

Jackie & Karl,
To Two People
Who Truly know
The Power of
God.
Enjoy.
Risë

xulon
PRESS

Consider It Done
by John, Ruth and Risë Pirinelli

Printed in the United States of America

ISBN 1-60034-448-8

www.xulonpress.com

CONTENTS

☆ ☆ ☆

DEDICATION

By John Pirinelli

As I fell to the ground after being shot by enemy small arms fire while on patrol with my army unit in Iraq, the first thought that came to my mind was, "I have to live for my son. God, please don't let me die." On the trip to the field hospital, my only wish was that the doctors would save my life so that I could always be there for my little boy.

It was at that moment, on July 28, 2004 at 11:40 p.m. near the city of Bayji, Iraq, that I felt the depth and intensity of the love I had for my unborn son. It is with that deep love that I dedicate this book to John Louis Pirinelli, Jr., born on October 25, 2004, and to my wonderful heavenly Father for giving me another chance at life.

John Louis Pirinelli, Jr.

AUTHOR'S NOTES

By Risë Pirinelli

The title of this book, *Consider It Done*, came from my deepest understanding of God's ways and His grace in our lives.

When John was injured in Iraq on July 28, 2004, during a firefight between the enemy and his army unit, the prognosis for his recovery from a near-fatal gunshot wound was dismal. His doctors speculated that if he lived, his recovery would take months. Would his duodenum and intestines heal, or would he live with a feeding tube and ileostomy for the rest of his life? Would he ever be able to eat again? Would he lose his other kidney that survived the initial injury? Would he need a kidney transplant? Would he have to be on dialysis for the rest of his life? Would he ever be weaned from the respirator?

John's rapid recovery appeared to be miraculous, and I stepped out in faith by saying it was so. However, John had many setbacks along the way.

Each day seemed like a lifetime as I watched him fight to beat the odds.

The weekend of September 25 and 26, 2004, was a particularly difficult one for me. John had yet another very serious setback, and I was weary. My legs and feet became heavier and heavier as I walked the quiet halls of Walter Reed Army Medical Center on that Sunday afternoon. I was trying to regain my strength so John would not know how upset I was.

I talked to God. "I'm so sorry, Lord. Did I misread what I thought to be signs from You and thus lead John and others astray? Was it just wishful thinking that John would have a complete recovery? Did I try to take over being You, instead of letting you be God, the Great Healer and Creator?"

As my mind whirled, He answered my questions, not audibly, but in a way that I heard in my mind and felt in my heart. "Consider it done."

"What, Lord, did you just tell me to consider it done? What does that mean? Do You mean that I should consider the miracle done, even though John is experiencing setbacks along the way?"

Again, God spoke to me. "Yes, Risë, consider it done." I was sure then of what I had heard.

With a renewed spirit and a spring in my step, I returned to John's hospital room with the strength only God can provide. John was "His child," and I would not question how He chose to heal John's body, mind, and spirit. What I would do now is believe God and trust His wonderful, loving ways. Without hesitation I would "consider it done."

FOREWORD

By New York State Senator
George D. Maziarz

Ruth Pirinelli found my home telephone number in the phone book. She called me on a Sunday afternoon — August 1, 2004 — and desperately told me she needed my help. I can still recall the anxiety in her voice when she described how her nephew, John, had just been seriously wounded in Iraq. John's brother, Philip, and his wife, Stephanie, wanted to travel to Germany to be with John, but they did not have passports. She asked if there was something I could do to expedite Philip and Stephanie's passport applications. Time was short, and something had to be done. And it was. After a startling series of events over a 16-hour time span, Philip and Stephanie obtained their passports and were at LaGuardia Airport in New York City awaiting their flight to Germany to support their wounded soldier.

I am convinced that Philip and Stephanie's sudden flight to Germany brought to John some of the best medicine he could have hoped for as he clung to life in a hospital bed. No obstacle in the logistics of the trip could stop them, though there were several. This is just one aspect of a much bigger story, yet even at that moment, it was clear that this family is strong enough, and their faith is strong enough, that nothing was going to stand in their way.

I was happy and relieved when I received an email from a nurse at Landstuhl Medical Center a few days later. She wrote that as soon as Philip and Stephanie arrived at John's bedside, the doctors witnessed a marked change for the better in John.

Today, by the grace of God, John and his young family are doing very well. Without question, John's unlikely recovery from life-threatening battle wounds can be considered nothing short of miraculous. Over the course of John's saga, the prayers of a loving family and an entire community were answered. It is an amazing story, and I am very glad the story is now a book that can be shared with the world.

May God continue to bless John, the Pirinelli family, and all those who sacrifice to defend our great nation.

INTRODUCTION

By Lieutenant Colonel Kyle M. McClelland
Commander, 1ˢᵗ Battalion
7ᵗʰ Field Artillery, 2d Brigade Combat Team
1ˢᵗ Infantry Division
Schweinfurt, Germany
10 July 2003 - 23 June 2005

As the battalion commander for Task Force 1-7 in Bayji, Iraq, from 4 February 2004 until 12 February 2005, I was responsible for over 750 soldiers, an Iraqi Army company of 120 and the day-to-day safety of over 450 civilians operating from Forward Operating Base Summerall in the northern portion of the contentious "Sunni Triangle." We had our good days, and we definitely had days that were not so good. During our year in Iraq, the "First Lightning" battalion suffered nine U.S. soldiers killed in action (KIA), over 30 Iraqi KIAs and numerous U.S. and Iraqi soldiers wounded in action (WIA), of which 13 U.S. WIA warriors would never return to active service due to the extent of their battle injuries.

One such warrior was Specialist John Pirinelli, Charlie Battery, 1st Battalion, 7th Field Artillery, who, on the night of 28 July 2004, sustained life-threatening gunshot wounds while engaged in a fire-fight with local insurgents. John's miraculous story continues from that night forward until today.

I visited John immediately following this enemy contact at the Combat Support Hospital in Tikrit. I had made such visits several times before, at all hours of the day and night, to check on both fatally and non-fatally injured soldiers. Like countless visits before, this one started with an ill feeling in my gut. When I walked into the Intensive Care Unit with my Command Sergeant Major Wayne Sanders, the doctors and nurses looked at us with saddened eyes… a look we had come to know all too well. I asked the head nurse, who had befriended us since our first visit to the Combat Support Hospital, to step outside and give us an honest assessment of John's condition. She provided us with a heart-breaking prognosis. John was seriously wounded, and his chances for survival were slim. She told us to keep praying. The doctors were going to stabilize John and move him to Baghdad for onward movement to Landstuhl, Germany, where he would receive specialized care and treatment.

I walked back into the ICU and was informed by one of the doctors that John had actually died earlier while in the operating room. This would be one of three times that "Big John" would medically expire, yet he continuously found a way to fight back and survive. He definitely was in the hands of a greater being whose vigilant watch and care of this warrior was an absolute miracle.

Throughout the next year, we followed John's incredible and miraculous medical recovery. His "Cobra" battle buddies, our entire chain of command, the medical personnel who treated him along the way, his loving and devoted family, and the people of Niagara Falls, New York, would stand strong and pray for John's recovery.

I kept in contact with John's family via email, and in each and every contact, the faith of his family would shine. "Please keep John in your prayers," his aunt would write. "He has a long road ahead, but he will survive. We have faith." And that is exactly what we did as we all were privileged to witness John's miraculous recovery.

We will never forget our fallen comrades and our band of brothers!!!

*John and LTC McClelland during a visit
in March 2006 to the Pentagon, LTC McClelland's
current assignment.*

THE TELEPHONE CALLS

by Risë

The ringing of the phone jarred me awake. I jumped out of bed, and even though my feet felt like lead, I ran to the kitchen to answer. My thoughts began to unfold. At this hour of the morning - 6:30 a.m. - this was either a wrong number or bad news. I told myself, as I told my son John before he went into the army and then to Iraq, I felt in my heart God would never take two of my children before he took me. I remembered the morning 13 years ago when I was nine months pregnant and went to the hospital to deliver what I already knew would be my still-born son. The heartache of losing my baby resurfaced unexpectedly as I tried to erase the negative thought from my mind that something terrible may have happened to John.

When your child is stationed in a war zone, your life as a civilian goes on, but subconsciously, you are always preparing for the worst. When John first told his father and I that he had received orders for Iraq, my reaction surprised even me. I felt peace when others around me felt despair. I began a "Monday morning habit" of visiting Father Baker's Basilica in Lackawanna, New York, on my way to work. Even though I am not Catholic, the Basilica is a magnificent cathedral and God's house, and I love it there. I would light candles and pray during my weekly visits. It is a place where I can come closer to God. Anytime I am carrying an especially heavy burden, I recall the story in the Bible about the woman who knew she would be healed if she could just touch the robe of Jesus. The Basilica is a place where I can touch the robe of Jesus.

With peace in my heart, I prayed unceasingly for the protection of not only my soldier, but for all the soldiers. Our family and friends placed reminders of John everywhere...American flags flew in the front yards of our homes; John's first army photo was displayed in our offices and homes; and magnetic yellow ribbons on our cars showed our support for not only John but for all the troops. Peace and pride surrounded all of us. We all believe only God knows when your child will come into this world and when that child will leave. All of the uncertainty in life can leave a gaping hole in one's existence. This hole can only be filled with faith in His divine wisdom and hope for the future if we are to continue on with productive and happy lives.

Answering the phone, I uttered the one simple word that caught in my throat. "Hello."

"This is Captain Lennox from the United States Army. May I speak to Mrs. Katrin Pirinelli, please?"

"Has something happened to John? This is his mother, Risë."

"I'm sorry, ma'am. I really need to speak to John's wife, Katrin."

An almost incapacitating wave of fear washed over me. This could not be good news. My worst fears had come true — but maybe not. With my mind reeling, I realized that if John had been killed, soldiers would be knocking on our door to give us the news.

Everyone in the house was sleeping. After all, our family had been very busy entertaining Katrin since she arrived from Germany for her first visit with us on July 16. I carried the cordless phone to Katrin. She was in a fragile state. She was six months pregnant with my grandson. She was lying on her side sleeping peacefully. I thought to myself how pretty she is with her 5' 2" stature and her short, blonde hair. I have often thought how sweet it is that my son John, at 6'6" and 290 pounds, chose such a petite wife. As I looked at her sleeping face, I pictured her beautiful smile, and my heart beat even faster as I realized that when she awoke, her smiling face would soon turn to one of sadness and tears. I woke her gently, and I handed her the phone. I was thinking how strange it was that I have been John's mother for 23 years, and I could not hear this news first. I rushed to the kitchen phone, picked it up and said, "Captain Lennox, this is Risë. I am listening. Is that okay?"

"Of course, Risë, I am just following procedures," replied the captain.

I braced myself for what I desperately wanted to know, but didn't want to hear.

"Mrs. Pirinelli, I have to inform you that your husband has been wounded in action. He was hit by enemy small arms fire at 11:40 p.m. last night while on patrol near Bayji. His liver has been grazed and his colon has been severed. He has lost one kidney, and has had one surgery. He is in a field hospital near Tikrit being cared for at this time. At last report, his condition is critical but stable."

Katrin was desperately trying to comprehend what she had just been told about her beloved, 23-year-old husband of six months. She knew what the captain was saying to her, but no words would come to her lips. Even though she was born and raised in Germany, she speaks English very well.

I grabbed paper and pen and wrote down everything the captain said. I was confused. How could John be in stable condition with injuries so severe? I decided I would not read anything into what the captain was telling us. I believe that one should not borrow trouble in life.

Finally Katrin asked, "Do you have any more information for me? Is he conscious? Does he know what has happened to him?"

"I haven't talked to him myself," the captain replied, "so I can't answer your questions. At this time, I am calling to let you know that John has been taken to a field hospital, and he is in very good hands. Our doctors and nurses are the best in the world. As soon as John is stabilized, he will be airlifted to Landstuhl Regional Medical Center in Germany. You will be hearing from me again as more information becomes available. Please try to stay calm."

"Captain Lennox, does John have all his extremities?" I asked with all my courage. I wanted to know, but I was so afraid of his answer.

"Yes, to my knowledge," the captain replied.

I didn't tell the captain this, but I was not convinced. As time went on, I would ask the same question over and over until I could see for myself.

Katrin and I hung up our phones. I walked back to the bedroom, and there was my husband, Bob, and Katrin sitting on the bed, holding each other and sobbing. We wondered if this was just a bad dream, but as the seconds ticked by, we knew that what we had just been told was very real. Little by little, the realization came to us that life as we knew it before we went to sleep just a few hours ago was over. A whole new life had just begun. Between her sobs and with tears running down her cheeks, Katrin told my husband and me that it seemed to her that, as Little John stirred inside her, he might be trying to tell her that she needed to stay calm and that his daddy was going to be okay.

Certainly the rest of the family needed to hear this news. My other son, Philip, and his wife, Stephanie, had to be told as well as my stepson, Rob, and his wife, Tracey, who live out of town. Tracey had heard a lot about John, but she had not met him. Now I wondered if she would ever know John.

I have always felt so blessed because Rob, Philip, and John are as close as brothers could be. Through their growing up years, they experienced all the fun brothers should; sports, hunting at our camp in Pennsylvania, playing cards, bonfires in our back yard with their friends, family vacations, and enjoying the family life that we treasured as we always tried to provide a Christian home for our children.

And Stephanie, well, she is more like a sister to John than a sister-in-law. When John was home on leave in December 2002, the two of them took advantage of several opportunities to have a great time together. Philip and Stephanie were disappointed when John could not be home for their wedding on June 15, 2002. John was on his first peacekeeping mission in Kosovo and was unable to get leave. Even though John was not at the wedding, he was still Philip's best man. In a taped message at their wedding reception, John gave the toast. "Philip, Stephanie, and everyone, this is Johnny. I hope everyone is having a real good time. I know I couldn't be there for the wedding, but part of being the best man is giving the toast. So this is for you. I couldn't let your wedding day go by without proposing a toast for the two best people in the world. Steph, I'm not bragging, but your husband, my brother, is definitely the best man in the world. He's everything anyone could want to be, and I know you love him, so please treat him the way he deserves to be treated. And, Phil, I couldn't have done a better job myself. Steph stands among the best, and I know she loves you. To the both of you, I'm sorry I can't be there, but you know I would be if I could. I pray that God will bless you and give you the children you deserve. So for now, everyone, have a great time. Let's toast Phil and Steph."

Following John's toast, the 200 wedding guests, amid the American flags waving in the guests' hands, sang aloud and heartfelt rendition of Lee Greenwood's "God Bless the USA" in John's honor. No, John was not forgotten, not for a minute, not in any place at any time or anywhere. He was always with us in thought, and he was always in our prayers.

My mother, John's Grandma Klein, also had to be told right away that John had been injured. She is a very important part of our family. After all, as we always remind her, if it weren't for her and my father, none of us would even be here, and none of us would ever have enjoyed the life in Christ we have if it wasn't for our parents.

Every Sunday, Mom and Dad took their three children, my brother, Roy, my sister, Ruth, and I, to Sunday school and church. We prayed before every meal and every night when we went to bed. Our parents taught us that without faith, life would be difficult and unhappy. And when we were grown, we all knew that the biggest gift we would give our own children would be the love of a Christian home and the faith that comes from knowing God and believing in His power.

Our beloved pastor, Rev. A. W. Moldenhauer of St. Matthew Lutheran Church in North Tonawanda, New York, where we have all worshipped for over 30 years, had taught us God always answers prayer, and He will not give us more than we can handle. Our first instinct was to beg God to save John. However, we all knew from praying the Lord's Prayer for years and years, it is God's will that would be done — nothing more and nothing less. It is all about God's will.

After these initial calls were made, many more followed. Ruth, Roy and his wife, Nyla, my husband's brother, Lou, and all the cousins had to be told. It wasn't long before the word had spread across the nation: "John Pirinelli had been shot in an exchange of gunfire with the enemy in Iraq. He was in a field hospital near Tikrit. Everyone should stand by for more information…and please, above all, please pray for John."

Before Katrin came to visit us, I made an appointment for her to have a sonogram during her visit. After her pre-natal tests in Germany in June, one of her tests, the alpha fetal protein, came back positive. She also had a sonogram in Germany, but it was inconclusive. If the test results were correct, the baby could possibly have Down Syndrome. She called us in near hysteria the day she received the results of the medical test. I have some medical knowledge from attending nursing school for three semesters, and other medical knowledge gained through my work as a social worker at an adult care facility. I knew many times medical tests give a false positive reading.

After Katrin's desperate phone call that day regarding the disheartening test results, just three weeks before John was injured, I once again felt the need to "touch the robe of Jesus," so I left work and made a pilgrimage to the Basilica. As I was returning to work with peace in my heart, my cell phone rang, and I knew who it was. I answered and heard John's somber voice. "Mom, what are we going to do?"

"John, I am returning to work from a visit to the Basilica, and I have peace of mind, the peace God

24

gives me when I need to be reminded that He knows everything happening in our lives. Remember John, God has a perfect plan for your life, and He has a perfect plan for your baby's life." And with that, I could hear the tension leave his voice. He had received the reassurance from me he needed, and he had strength to carry on. Little did we know that in 25 days, our lives would change dramatically, and we would be wondering if John would even be alive for the birth of his child.

A few days after that conversation with John, I received this email from him, written on July 5, 2004 at 9:07 p.m. "Hey, Mom, how are you. I am good. I miss you very much. I have been trying to stay positive about the baby, but I am just scared. I don't know the first thing about taking care of a handicapped child, and all I ever wanted was a family with healthy, normal children. Well, I know you will, but please keep lighting candles and praying. With everything I am going through in Iraq, it has no comparison to the fear I have over this. I would gladly give my own life so the baby would be healthy. Well, My Mother, I have to get some sleep. I will call when I can. I love you."

Katrin needed to have the sonogram before she went back home to Germany. The family was having a baby shower for Katrin on Friday. The upcoming weekend was our annual cousins' reunion. What were we going to do? How were we going to go on? Should we go on?

We did go on. Katrin and I arrived at the doctor's office at 9:30 a.m. Shortly thereafter, as I saw my grandson in his mother's womb for the very first time, I couldn't help but wonder if this precious new life was going to begin with the burden of not having a father. On the other hand, I did thank God at that moment that my son, Little John's father, had become everything I had ever hoped he would be. It was possible that John was going to make the ultimate sacrifice for his country. Amidst all my fear and sadness, I was filled with pride. But, in the back of my mind, I felt tremendous doubt about John's condition. As a mother, the sixth sense I had developed when it comes to my children was giving me the feeling that John's condition was much worse than we were being told. Once again, I went over in my mind the conversation with Captain Lennox. Then I convinced myself I could be of more use to my son if I stayed calm. Every chance I got, I prayed for a miracle for John.

After the sonogram was finished, Katrin and I left the doctor's office and went to the video store to have a DVD made of the sonogram. Katrin was excited. She couldn't wait to show it to John, although she was not sure when or where that would be. It appeared our little baby was in good health and was perfectly developed. To say we were thankful did not seem to fully express our relief and gratitude. Katrin was suddenly quiet, and then she asked, "Mom, what if John's condition is worse than we are being told?"

With all the reassurance I could muster, I said, "Katrin, John is going to be okay. He is receiving wonderful medical care, and hopefully, by Saturday, he will arrive at the hospital in Germany. I have heard the hospital there for the wounded soldiers is state-of-the-art, and its medical staff deals with injuries like John's every day. They know what to do. They will have him patched up in no time." In my mind, I hoped I was convincing her because, at intermittent unexpected moments, I was having a hard time convincing myself. Little did I know then that John was receiving unit after unit of blood in the effort to keep him alive.

After we arrived home, I checked the answering machine. Our friends and family were calling us to find out how John was. Captain Lennox had our cell phone numbers, so we knew we hadn't missed a call from him. Some of our closest friends brought food for us. I was already overwhelmed at the support we were receiving since we learned just that morning that John was injured. Katrin called Captain Lennox for an update on John's condition. He had nothing new to report. We tried to rest, but already we could feel the exhaustion overtaking us. After the day ended, we placed our heads on our pillows, prayed for a miracle for John, and also prayed that we would not be awakened by a telephone call or visited by soldiers the next day to tell us that John had died.

The next morning, when I awoke and opened my eyes, I instantly thought about John. "Thank you, God." John must still be alive. I would have known in my heart if he wasn't. It seemed like climbing Mt. Everest would be easier than facing today's trials. The phone was ringing already, and it was only 9:00 a.m.

Friends and family were calling for news on John's condition. The latest report we had received was that the doctors had performed a second surgery as they continued to repair the damage to John's internal organs from the gunshot wound. I determined to keep myself busy and positive, and hopefully the day would pass by quickly. Katrin called Captain Lennox once again to find out how John was doing after his second surgery. John was still with us on earth. There was no change in his condition. We prepared for Katrin's baby shower. I marveled at everyone around us as I saw faith in action. We would continue to believe that John was going to be all right. A little doubt slipped in, and I immediately erased it.

When we arrived at Phil and Stephanie's home for the baby shower, the setting was just perfect. The Winnie the Pooh theme was just what Katrin loves. Those who are close to us were there. We were all trying to be happy and upbeat for Katrin and each other. She received beautiful gifts for the baby, and soon the evening ended. We were all worn out. Before we left and as a group, we once again asked God to continue to heal John's body. We had no reason to believe this was not exactly what was happening at that very moment.

Within an hour, we were home and trying to get some sleep. We would follow the same routine every night when we went to bed — lay our heads on our pillows and ask God for a miracle for John, and we would also ask that if army officials called, it would be to give us good news. And more than anything else, we continually prayed with all our might that soldiers would not appear at the front door of our home.

Saturday morning arrived and we hadn't received any updated news about John. Once again we reminded ourselves that no news was good news. Katrin was going home to Germany today. After we dressed, we put her belongings in the car and returned to Phil and Steph's. The cousins' reunion started today. It was good to see our family and very comforting to us as we waited for news about John. After a few hours, it was time to take Katrin to the airport. We gathered in a huge circle to pray. We asked God for Katrin's safe return to Germany and for her strength when she got there. Hopefully, she would be seeing her injured husband in a few hours, and we knew how difficult this would be for her.

Before we began our prayer, my cell phone rang. First Sergeant Ebbs, John's First Sergeant when he was stationed at Schweinfurt, was calling from Germany. "Good news," he said. "John is leaving Iraq now on a medical transport plane. He should arrive at Landstuhl in the middle of the night." This was another blessing to thank God for. We thought it was God's plan once again that Katrin and John would both arrive in Germany within hours of each other. Army personnel would pick Katrin up at the airport and take her directly to the hospital, Landstuhl Regional Medical Center, where John was being taken. This would be a bittersweet reunion for Katrin and John. Katrin would be so thrilled to see John, but if she had a choice, of course, she would rather he was in Iraq, healthy and whole. She realized the choice was not up to her, and she would somehow cope with John's injury and the new hand life had dealt her.

Katrin shared a tearful farewell with her new extended family, and my husband and I took her to the airport. During the half-hour ride, we dug down into ourselves as deep as we could and gave her all the hope and encouragement we could gather. She was 22 years old and pregnant, returning to her homeland to hold a vigil by her wounded husband's side. She was going to need all the help she could get. After she was checked in and comfortable at the airport, we left her at the gate with heavy hearts.

We had no sooner returned to the party when Katrin called. She was about to leave Buffalo for Detroit and had just been told by airline personnel they doubted she would make her connecting flight in Detroit that would take her to Frankfurt where army personnel would be waiting for her to take her to John. In a panic, we returned to the airport to see if we could find an airport employee who could contact the airport in Detroit in an effort to work out a plan that would get Katrin on her flight to Frankfurt.

I ran to Security, with my shoes in my hand, begging passengers to let me pass by them, and they did. I wanted so badly to reach Katrin's gate before her plane took off so I could tell her that I would do everything possible to make sure she made her connection. The security personnel checked me thoroughly and gave me the okay to continue on. I proceeded to the gate, only to find out that Katrin's plane had taken off.

Gathering my breath and my thoughts, I asked to speak with a supervisor. I pleaded with the supervisor as I told him Katrin's circumstances and why she must make her connection in Detroit. "Please, we need your help. My son, Katrin's husband, has been wounded in Iraq. He is on a medical transport plane bringing him from Iraq to Landstuhl Regional Medical Center in Germany. Katrin needs to get there as soon as possible. There is no time to waste. She must make that connection in Detroit for her flight to Frankfurt. Is there something you can do to help?"

The kind supervisor heard my pleas. As one of the first compassionate Americans we would encounter during the next few months, he called the airport in Detroit and made arrangements for a driver with a cart to be at the gate to pick Katrin up when she arrived in Detroit and take her to her connecting flight. It was no surprise to any of us when we found out later all had gone well and as planned, and Katrin made her connection to Frankfurt. Katrin commented later she certainly did feel like a VIP. If we had known then what we know now, this would be the first of many, many times we would be made to feel like celebrities. I can humbly say now that my son, my hero, was a celebrity not only in our eyes but also in the eyes of all Americans who knew him, and multitudes who didn't.

With this hurdle behind us, we returned to Phil's and rejoined the family reunion. It was so quiet and peaceful at Phil and Steph's country home. There was plenty of good food, a campfire, and games for the kids, including a bounce house even the adults were enjoying. On the surface, everything seemed so normal. Anyone on the outside looking in would never have been able to guess what was really going on in our hearts and minds. Everyone was so grateful to be together. We didn't even notice the clouds in the sky. It was a rainy day, and at times I thought those soft raindrops were actually tears from heaven caused by the pain my son was going through at that very moment.

As I sat back and tried to relax for a while, I thought, "How can I be here, at a long-anticipated and happy event like a family reunion, at the same time my son is lying in a hospital bed thousands of miles away from home with a gunshot wound in his stomach?" I later learned that everyone there was thinking the same thing. We were all trying to be strong for each other, but we were all so frightened. The only place any of us could have found a measure of comfort would have been right next to John's hospital bed.

After the rain stopped, we sat around the campfire and talked about John, and the setting seemed perfect. There were at least 30 of us sitting in a big circle, baking "hobo pies," one of our family's favorite foods, on the hot coals and helping the children roast their marshmallows. The sky had cleared, the stars were out, and the bright moon showed us the heavens. We reminisced about John as a young boy, about the day he left home and went into the army, and we shared all the stories he told us about life in the military. We laughed as we recalled his antics. There were also tears of grief and sadness as we let the foreboding feeling sink into our hearts and minds, a little bit at a time, that John's condition could be much worse than we were being told.

When the party ended a few hours later, we said our goodbyes. We were all exhausted from the emotional strain of the day. We all knew getting a good night's sleep would be almost impossible, and we looked forward to being together again in the morning. Once again, I feared that when I closed my eyes and went to sleep, the telephone ringing or soldiers knocking on my front door might awaken me. I decided I would continue to trust God and pray for a miracle for John.

When I think back now to the activities of the cousins' reunion and everything that transpired, there was no doubt it was all part of "God's Plan." Most of the family was in attendance and had come from as far away as New Jersey and Florida for this very special annual event. The baby shower for Katrin showed the generosity of our friends and family. When Saturday night came, we knew we had made the right decision by continuing on with our plans. After all, it gave us a great opportunity to pray for John in a large group, and we did.

The phone rang early the next morning as Bob and I were getting ready for church. It was Dr. Shorr, John's primary doctor, calling from Landstuhl Regional Medical Center. John had arrived at Landstuhl in Germany, and Dr. Shorr broke the news to us that John's condition was grave. His remaining kidney was barely functioning, and he might need dialysis. A respirator was breathing for him, and his oxygen level was a mere 40%. He had lost a lot of blood. His blood pressure was dangerously low. His body was filling with fluid. John had exploratory surgery after arriving at Landstuhl that had revealed many other complications. Dr. Shorr explained that because John's body had been so severely traumatized by his injuries, he had gone into shock. John had also developed sepsis, an infection in his blood. Dr. Shorr told us it was urgent that we get to John's bedside as quickly as possible. The army would make the arrangements. I would find out later that Dr. Shorr had written in John's chart that day, "Patient has severe injuries, and likelihood of survival is uncertain." This was what Dr. Shorr was trying to tell me as gently as he could, and I heard exactly what he was saying.

Dr. Shorr asked me if I would please take just a few minutes and talk with Sergeant Rodas, John's social worker, who would make the arrangements for us to travel to Germany. Even though I was very anxious to get to church, I suspended my thoughts about church momentarily as I realized that Sergeant Rodas would be a key figure in quickly getting us to Germany. Sergeant Rodas and I discussed the travel arrangements. When we finished, I asked Sergeant Rodas to give John a message from my husband and me. "Please tell John we are on our way to church right now, and we will be praying for him. We will see him soon. Please tell him we love him." I wanted to remind John that he is a soldier and a fighter, and that he just might be fighting the biggest and most important battle of his life right now, but I decided I would tell him that when I could be with him in person. Sergeant Rodas told me he would talk to me later in the day, and then he assured me he would go to see John as soon as we hung up. Much, much later I would learn that even though Sergeant Rodas gave John my message, he had serious doubts John heard it.

I hung up the phone, and my husband and I left for church, almost in a robotic state. When we arrived at church, I had no memory of the five-mile trip we had just taken to get there, but I was aware that the sun was shining, and the warmth of its rays was comforting. My husband found our pastor in his vestry and told him of John's deteriorating condition. Pastor Moldenhauer baptized John as a baby and confirmed him at age 14. He knew John well. "Johnny," as he called him. And so, during the service on that bright, sunny morning, August 1, 2004, Pastor led the congregation in song. We sang "Amazing Grace," requested by me, and "Onward Christian Soldiers," requested by my son, Philip.

Only three days earlier, on the day that we'd received the news John had been injured, Philip called Pastor Moldenhauer and asked him if they could meet at church. "Of course," Pastor said, "I'll be right there." During their conversation, Philip told him, in a choked-up voice so low he could hardly be heard and with tears in his eyes, "Pastor, I wish the bullet would have hit me. But I know my brother is a Christian. He is a Christian soldier. I can't even go see him. Can we sing 'Onward Christian Soldiers' in church?" Pastor made sure we did.

When we finished singing the songs, Pastor led the congregation in prayer. "We thank you, Holy Father, that we could have one more Sunday to get ready for eternal life. Bless all the military from this congregation who are in Afghanistan and Iraq. Especially do we ask your blessings upon Johnny — Johnny Pirinelli. We offer him before you to strengthen his faith as he learned it in confirmation class, and that surely goodness and mercy shall follow him. Bless his mom and dad who are keeping a prayerful vigil and his wife, great with child, that Johnny can be around when that baby is born; that the family does not give up, but is strengthened in their prayer moments. Bless this congregation with the awareness to keep praying for Johnny, not only today, but tomorrow and the next day. Bless the hands of the surgeons and their minds that they may be skillful and perfect in whatever they have to do. Bless the reunion of Johnny and his parents when they arrive at his bedside in Germany. Into thy hands we commend him and them, and bless their attendance here at the Table in a few moments. And whatever else we need to be practicing Christians, we include in the prayer, Dear Jesus, which you taught us to pray." Then we prayed the Lord's Prayer.

When Pastor began to deliver his sermon, he looked out into the congregation and saw the tears of our fellow parishioners, the people with whom we had worshipped for years, the families of the children John had grown up with. He reminded everyone that even Jesus wept when Lazarus died. "It is okay to cry. Just remember to keep praying for Johnny."

After Pastor Moldenhauer's sermon was finished, I walked to the altar to take communion, and when I returned to the pew, I collapsed ...and I prayed. I had just received the forgiveness of my sins from God, and now I was asking Him to please, please save my son's life.

When we returned home after church, the house began filling with concerned friends and relatives. Neighbors brought food. My dear friends, Diane Adamek and Sue Breier, packed my suitcase. I remember almost every moment of that day. As I wandered from room to room, it became a day of tears, hugs, and the quiet presence of those close to us who sometimes didn't know what to say.

As the day unfolded, we received many telephone calls from army officials as our travel arrangements were completed. Philip and Stephanie wanted to go to Germany to be with John, but they didn't have passports. Everyone knew it took a minimum of three weeks to get passports. Phil and Steph couldn't wait. I was vaguely aware of events that were transpiring as my sister, Ruth, received help from New York State Senator George Maziarz in the effort to get passports for Phil and Steph.

After a very hectic day full of emotional ups and downs, the sun set. It was Sunday night and time to go to bed.

I was physically and emotionally exhausted as I recalled one other time in my life when my burdens were so unbearable. It was the night before I delivered my stillborn son, Louis, who died in my womb through an umbilical cord accident. Two of my sons, Baby Louis and John, with all the love and fullness they brought into my life, had also, through no fault of their own, left me with an emptiness in my soul I felt at that moment I would never recover from. My heart had been broken when I lost my baby, Louis, whom I adored throughout my pregnancy, and my heart was breaking now with the injury of my son, John.

My sister, Ruth, was worried about Bob and me, and so she decided to spend the night with us. Even though she did not say so, I knew she was staying with us because she was afraid we might receive bad news about John's condition, and she didn't want us to be alone if that happened.

The moment I laid my head on my pillow, a panic attack overtook my body with the force of a huge tidal wave. Even my sister, who knows me well, could not calm me. I was inconsolable. Ruth was alarmed and insisted she was going to call my doctor and ask for tranquilizers for me. The agony and fear in her voice made me realize it was not just me who was suffering. I began to quiet myself down, and I assured Ruth that I did not need drugs to calm my nerves and control my waves of panic. I would use prayer in place of drugs. We began to pray for peace and a miracle for John. Within moments, I closed my eyes and gave my grief to Jesus. There was no way I could travel this path without Him. The Lord's peace flooded my soul so completely that this incident would prove to be the last time throughout this whole ordeal that I would panic.

We slept for a few hours, and before we knew it we were waking up to a new day, Monday, August 2, 2004, feeling a mixture of nervousness and anticipation, but surely holding in our hearts the promise our pastor reminded us of in church the day before, that Jesus would help us carry our cross. When we left our home for the airport to begin our journey to

Germany, little did we know that we would not return home for many weeks. We arrived at the airport and checked in. We went through Security and walked down the hallway to our gate. With each step I took, I found the strength to take another. I was getting closer to my son.

The thought of John lying in a bed critically wounded and so many thousands of miles from home was almost more than I could bear. I couldn't be with him to hold his hand or soothe his pain, but I knew one thing for sure: that God was taking care of John, and His guardian angels were with John. The best thing we could do was pray for John, and so we did.

"God, You already know John is hurt. And, God, You know he believes and knows You are with him. He knows You will take care of him. Many years ago, on July 20, 1981, when You gave John to us, we knew there were no promises as to how long we might have him here on earth. God, I'm not ready to give my son up yet, but if it is Your will, I will accept it. But, please, Lord, if it is at all possible, I am asking for a miracle, that John will live and be whole again, in body, mind, and soul."

Throughout my life I have professed my faith in God and my love for Jesus Christ. In my early teenage years I became intrigued with miracles, and as a young adult I learned they really could happen. Clearly, this new journey I began from the moment John was shot was going to be the ultimate test of my faith. I was now committed to give back to God more than ever, and to become a soldier myself as my son clung to life. God placed His loving arms around me and gave me the peace I needed to live what I believed. From the time I made my first request to God for a miracle for John, I believed in my heart that if God had chosen to talk to me at that moment, He would have said, "Consider it done."

JOINING THE ARMY

by Risë

As most mothers do when they give birth, I, too, will never forget the "birth day" of my child. My labor and delivery were very easy when John was born. As I looked at him peacefully sleeping in his little nursery bed, I thought to myself that surely someone would think he was a girl because he was so beautiful. I quickly found out I wasn't the only person who noticed his exceptional beauty. The nurses kept remarking about how gorgeous he was. His features were perfect in every way, and he was a precious bundle of flawlessness and happiness from God. John's two older brothers, Phil and Rob, my stepson, thought their baby brother was a new toy to play with, and my husband and I were excited to take John home from the hospital. We had once again been blessed with a healthy, new son, and we thanked God over and over.

From the day we brought John home he displayed his distinctive personality. One moment he was smiling, the next he was screaming with the pain of colic. Eight months later and after several attempts at different formulas, I was finally able to find a formula that agreed with John. I began to see more smiles and fewer tears. His personality wasn't clouded with pain anymore, and he became the toy his brothers had been waiting for. He was a very happy and contented baby, and he was right on target with his development. He walked when he was 11 months old. He was saying many words at 14 months. Physically he was off the charts. He was very agile, even at a young age. I was thankful for that because he was so big. Most of his visits to the doctor were for his regular check-ups. Bouts with illness were few and far between. He was extremely strong, and little did I know that God was sculpting my son into a strong soldier.

John loved to watch TV. His favorite television program when he was very young was Mr. Dress-Up. He would sit in front of the TV with pretzels, his favorite snack. My husband and I decided I would be a stay-at-home mom. Our lives were built on God, family, friends, and the activities of three children. Being the baby of the family, John would learn many life lessons from his older brothers.

We would regularly attend Boy Scout activities with Rob and help him deliver his newspapers. Being the older brother, Rob loved to spoil John. When John was being disciplined, I would see Rob trying to save him from his punishment. John always looked up to Rob, and they never considered the fact they were half brothers.

Philip, on the other hand, being only four years older than John and the middle child, was not as tolerant of John. When John was first born, Philip started suffering from excruciating stomachaches. When Phil became secure with his position in the family, his stomachaches abruptly and mysteriously stopped. As Philip and John grew with Rob watching over both of them, I would see the daily competition between them for my attention. After awhile, though, and at very young ages, they all learned they had a special place in my heart, and each of them developed a unique relationship with me.

Eventually, John would let Phil and Rob take on the role of the older brothers. John willingly accepted Phil's advice and Rob's guidance. John was a very smart boy, and he managed to reap the benefits of having two older brothers to not only learn from, but to also convince they should do his chores for him. His brothers would eventually teach him how to ride a bike, fish, play ball, camp, spot deer, and hunt. Little did we know then that someday John would teach them bravery beyond anything they could have ever known.

The hustle and bustle of a growing family made John's "baby years" fly by. It wasn't long before John was three years old. He went to Sunday school and nursery school. He was a "mama's boy," and he would cling to me when I said goodbye to him at school. Soon, though, he was off playing with his little friends. He earned the "Best Personality Award" in nursery school, and this was proof he was enjoying his life outside his home. John's sweet personality was shining.

When it was time for John to go to kindergarten, he was ready. He continued to make friends, and his report cards were something to be proud of. At five years old, John was, without a doubt, the most pampered child in our household.

St. Matthew Lutheran School in North Tonawanda, New York, was a wonderful place for my children to go to school. Not only did they learn reading, writing, and arithmetic, they also received religious education every day. My husband and I felt this part of our children's education would be their best preparation for the circumstances life would present to them.

John's development continued, and an active little boy emerged. His teachers commented about all of his abilities, but he didn't put his best effort into his schoolwork. His annual achievement tests would show he excelled in "Social Environment," "Vocabulary," and "Language," yet he seemed to be more interested in playing than in doing his work. His keen intuition, ability to see through people, and sensitive nature would expose him to many of the harsh realities of life. At times, these realizations would overwhelm and confuse him. Hence, the root cause of his feelings that sometimes life just wasn't fair.

As John grew, at times I would see his strong will overcome his mild nature. My heart would ache as I wondered how he was going to get through life and get along with people when, at times, he could be so obstinate. I hoped his sweet nature would help him overcome his stubbornness.

John played little league baseball and basketball. He also took piano and guitar lessons, and he enjoyed Boy Scouts. Some of the best times he had were on his walks through the woods with his dad, who taught him to enjoy nature and the wonder of God's creations. We bought a four-wheeler for our boys, and John looked forward to the day he could be the driver instead of the passenger. Zuccari Farms, a large dairy farm, operated across the street from our home, and some of our boys' fondest memories were from their adventures on the farm.

John was very close to his maternal and paternal grandparents. Because they lived close by, he saw them weekly. Each of them brought a unique joy to his life. Grandpa Klein and John enjoyed watching TV together, especially Magnum, or "Magum," as John would call it. Grandpa and John would sit on the couch with Grandpa's arm around John, and John would look at his grandpa's strong hands with admiration.

Grandma Klein would prepare John's favorite foods for him — macaroni and cheese and Cheese Whiz sandwiches with ketchup. She made sure she had his favorite snacks of pretzels, cheese puffs, and pickles on hand every time he visited. He would relish the times Grandma Klein would caress his feet as she would wash the dirt off them in the sink.

Grandma Pirinelli would order pizza before John came to her house, and he looked forward to sharing that special treat with her. Grandpa Pirinelli would make a funny face with his lips, scrunching his upper lip to the right and his lower lip to the left, and later on John would learn to imitate his grandpa's funny face so he could tease people just like his grandpa did.

John's grandparents added so much to John's life in a very positive way, and they loved John just the way he was. He was sure to display his sweetness to his grandparents, and his stubbornness was well hidden from them.

My children were fortunate to have cousins to grow up with who lived close by. My sister's children, Risë (named after me), Kristy, and Dawn, and my brother's children, Tim, Mike, and Jeff, were more like brothers and sisters to John than cousins. We all spent a lot of time together. We enjoyed birthday parties for each child, holidays, and vacations. Together, the three families established traditions we hoped would last for generations. Our children learned the obligations that came with being part of a family and always doing what is right for each individual in their lives.

The most important events we all shared were at St. Matthew where our children were baptized and confirmed, and where they attended school through eighth grade. Every Sunday morning started with anticipation of the cousins, grandparents, aunts, and uncles being together in church. To say we were blessed does not seem to be an adequate description of what our children gained from having a close and loving extended family.

John was the youngest for quite a few years until his cousin, Dawn, came along. As John was ousted from his position as the "baby of the family," he became resentful of Dawn. Their relationship was intense, all the way from watching TV together as buddies to fighting with each other. Sometimes they would join forces in an effort to either gain something they wanted or escape the penalty for something they did wrong. Eventually, though, they each found their place, and they became great friends.

Cousin Kristy and John were the most alike in personality even though they were four years apart in age. They both struggled with feeling the pressure to conform to others' expectations of them. Everyone in the family was prepared to expect the unexpected from them as they grew up. They developed an unspoken language between them, and this bond would help them pull off their pranks. They fiercely defended each other when their guilt was exposed.

I can't help but chuckle when I remember everyday events of John's youth. When he was very young, he would watch me put my makeup on in the morning, and he would tell me he didn't like it. "Mom, I love you just the way you are," he would say. He loved to play a game at bedtime called "kiss wipe off." I would kiss him, and he would wipe it off, and then I would have to kiss him again. If John had his wish, "kiss wipe off" would have extended into the wee hours of the morning. If he would cry, he would make me promise I wouldn't tell anyone. This was my sweet son, John. One of John's trademarks was his consistent reaction when he was disciplined. His cute little face would scowl, and with crossed arms and a pout, he would tell me, "It's not fair."

There came a time when I would tell him, "I know, John, it's not fair," before he had a chance to tell me.

Some of our fondest memories are from special times spent at our camp in Pennsylvania. There the boys could run and play. They learned gun safety and how to hunt. Their father taught them the names of all the different species of birds and other wildlife, and the excitement would build at dusk when they would make their preparations to spot deer. When they came back to the camp, we would build a huge campfire and eat Reuben sandwiches, pizza, roasted corn, and hobo pies. Relatives lived close by, and we enjoyed our visits with them. We established many family traditions in Pennsylvania that we hoped our boys would enjoy for years to come.

John began his confirmation classes at St. Matthew in seventh grade. Every school day would start with our pastor teaching the students about God, the Bible, and our Savior, Jesus Christ. Every day for these children was preparation for the rest of their lives. John was taught that God would always take care of him and that he needed to have faith in that belief. Pastor also taught John all the reasons why he needed to believe in God and where he could find the proof in the Bible. With all his heart, John did believe, and he was confirmed at the end of eighth grade.

In addition to participating in sports and Boy Scouts, John also tried acting. Philip was Tevye in *Fiddler on the Roof* when John was in eighth grade. John enjoyed his own part in the same musical. Although he wasn't the star of the show, he was very proud of his brother, who was. As a matter of fact, we would see something in John as he was growing up that was an asset. He was very humble, and he would willingly let someone else be in the limelight, although he was growing into a jokester who liked to make people laugh. (Sometimes his foolish behavior worked against him and got him into trouble when he was supposed to be paying attention in school!)

John really looked forward to going to high school at Niagara Wheatfield HS in Sanborn, New York. There he would play football, basketball, and lacrosse. Because of his size and agility, he was a good athlete. However, it wasn't long before he experienced some of the politics of high school sports, and he became discouraged and quit. He needed to do something with his spare time, and so he began working at a local pizzeria as a cook and then eventually as a delivery person.

John began to show signs of rebelliousness in tenth grade. His teachers liked him, but it appeared that he thought his way of doing things was the preferred way over what his teachers expected of him. My husband and I made many trips to school as we worked with John's teachers and tried to impress upon John the importance of his education. However, he had different ideas about where his life was going, and his priorities switched from school to his friends and having fun. We tried to tell him these were the best years of his life, and he should work hard in school, but our coaxing was to no avail. He had other ideas. While John never got into any serious trouble in school, he struggled socially. In the end, he did graduate. He had grown from my blonde-haired, brown-eyed, handsome little boy into my blonde-haired, brown-eyed, handsome young man.

I was elated when John received his high school diploma. As part of his graduation celebration, I presented him with a poem I had written for him:

HOW DO WE KNOW?

Dear John,
How do we know
> *What life has in store?*
Or how do we show
> *Our children to soar?*
What does it take
> *To succeed in this life?*
How do we spare our child
> *The ache caused by strife?*
The answer is clear.
> *Yes, very deep in my heart.*
Pray, hope, love, and hear,
> *And let God do His part.*
I know this is true.
> *Let me tell you why it's so.*
One rarely feels blue when we
> *Do our best and "let go."*
So...John, take my advice.
> *Keep God in your heart*
And believe in yourself.
> *You'll succeed from the start.*

Love, Mom

After graduation, John went to work for a black-top sealing and coating company. He continued to be the comic relief no matter where he was or whom he was with. Making people laugh was something he was really good at. However, he began to realize that unless he could make a living doing it, being a comedian wasn't going to feed him or, eventually, a family. As parents who wanted more for their son, we argued with him and tried to point out to him he needed to do something more with his life. His stubbornness took over once again, and he turned a deaf ear to us. As we became more frustrated with him in our efforts to encourage him to start finding a more productive direction for his life, he became more distant. He always remained very respectful to us, and he would check in regularly when he wasn't at home. But we were worried about him. He was floundering, and that was breaking my heart.

After a series of unproductive events in John's life, I delivered an ultimatum to him. He had two weeks to find another place to live. He had already enrolled in college, but it was clear he was not ready to focus on school. I sat back and wondered what his choice was going to be.

A few days after my ultimatum to John, he came home and sat down in the rocking chair with a very serious look on his face. After we finished dinner, he called me into another room. "Mom, I don't want you to tell anyone what I am going to tell you. I just left the recruiter, and I think I'm going to join the army." I told him I thought that was the best decision he had made in a long time. He needed the structure of the military to get his life back on a productive tract. Before the evening was over, he was telling everyone his news, and this sealed his commitment to this new adventure. He went back to the recruiter's office the next day to pick up the paperwork that had to be completed. When he returned it to the recruiter's office, he was told he would be leaving for basic training in ten days. While a lot of recruits have a delayed enlistment, John realized he had wasted enough time. He was moving ahead with his new life. This time his stubbornness would work to his advantage, and my sweet, gentle giant of a son was going to do something to make all of us very proud of him. He would have preferred we reserve our pride and admiration for him until he had proven himself, but in our eyes, before he had even gone to basic training, he had shown us his courage and bravery. I knew in my heart he was going to make a good soldier.

Just like the day he was born, the day John left for basic training is one I will never forget. It seemed like an eternity ago I was so worried about him and his future. And now, here he was, entering the military and beginning the process of finding his own way in life. I told John many times when he was growing up that he would have just himself and God, and that he may as well give in to the fact that God would have His way with him. Now, as he left home, I knew God would take care of John for me, and this was the best choice John could make for himself.

When John arrived at basic training at Fort Sill, Oklahoma, he called me. During our small talk, I could sense his fear about his new life as I listened to his quivering voice. I reminded him he was in good hands, and nothing was going to happen to him that he and God could not take care of together. He seemed to calm down a bit, and then we had to hang up. During the next 16 weeks, I talked to him only a few times. Those telephone calls were very short, and I tried to pack as much into them as I could without overwhelming him. I taped a few of our telephone conversations on my answering machine. I took that tape out of the machine after John left basic training, and I vowed to save it for the rest of my life.

While John was in basic training, our family members encouraged John every chance they could. One of us would write a silly poem, and then we would all send it to him, along with our own words of support. Sometimes he would receive ten letters from home at one time.

At family gatherings, we would talk about how he might be reacting when he received these letters from home. We could picture him very clearly — a big, strapping, soldier reading goofy poetry with a sweet smile on his face. John told us later how he laughed at his silly family and how this lifeline from home helped him get through the tough times of basic training.

On October 31, 2001, Bob and I, Philip, Stephanie, and my mother attended John's graduation from basic training at Fort Sill, Oklahoma. We were so proud that he had successfully completed the first phase of his military career. All the pomp and ceremony that was surrounding our son, who looked so handsome in his uniform, brought tears of happiness to our eyes. At dinner that night, I presented John with another poem I had written for him based on "Operation Enduring Freedom," the name of the United States military's response to the September 11, 2001, terrorist attacks on the United States:

FREEDOM TO ENDURE

She sits in the crowd
    A smile on her face.
She praises God how
    They progressed to this place.
Surrounded by loved ones
    The "freedom" to just be.
Overflowing pride for a son
    She knows the world can see.
She remembers back 20 years
    The day that he was born.
And even though she held him near
    His lost innocence she would mourn.
Three days ago she completed 50 years
    Half of these, a mother and a wife.
Her family and friends always near
    Questioned how to celebrate her life.
The Master had a perfect plan
    The celebration, time and place
At Sheridan Theater, with a uniformed man
    And now she would see his face.
At 10:00 a.m. he enters the room
    His residence, an army base.
Forever forgotten any gloom
    Her son "Endured" and won the race.

54

His mother knew the risk of his calling
Her son knew he would always be secure
Because they know life is not for falling
God will give John the "FREEDOM TO
ENDURE."

Love, Mom

So many times in the last few years, I prayed, thanking God for John and who he was, stubbornness, sweetness and all. I knew God had molded John into the man He wanted him to be, and now John would be my blonde-haired, brown-eyed, handsome soldier. I asked God to set John on a path that would bring purpose and peace to his life and make him an extraordinary soldier. With all the events of the past few months and the progress I was seeing my son make, I could clearly sense God's answer to John and to me, "Consider it done."

PREPARING FOR BATTLE

by John

☆ ☆ ☆

July 10, 2001, was a big day for me. This was the day I entered the army. My recruiter picked me up at my home to take me to the airport. My mother, father, and grandmother also went to the airport with us and were there to send me off on this new adventure. Private John R. Pirinelli — I could hardly believe it. As I look back now, I felt a lot of emotion, but no fear. I was ready. My parents made sure my brothers and I were involved in lots of activities during our growing-up years, including Boy Scouts, sports, and church, so they had done a very good job of preparing me for the real world. I left my home that day, ready to begin a new chapter in my book of life. Mom had "armed" me with a guardian angel medal I would always keep in my pocket. It would be that guardian angel that would ultimately give me the courage I would need to be a good soldier, a soldier my fellow soldiers could depend on, no matter what.

I received my basic training and Advanced Individual Training (AIT) at Fort Sill, Oklahoma. I distinctly remember September 11, 2001. My unit was in a field training exercise when our superiors told us passenger airplanes hijacked by terrorists had smashed into the Twin Towers in New York City and the Pentagon, and it was suspected another plane had been hijacked and had crashed in Pennsylvania. We didn't believe it. Initially we thought this was part of the mental conditioning you go through in basic training. When we returned to our barracks a few days later, we were stunned and saddened to learn that this horrible news was true. We talked about it for hours, but never did we think this event would result in war.

I finished my basic training, and on November 1, 2001, I went to Airborne Training at Fort Benning, Georgia. During this time, all I could think about was 9/11. I watched the news whenever I could.

During a training exercise at Ft. Benning, I suffered stress fractures in my left foot. That ended my training at Ft. Benning, and I knew that shortly I would be receiving orders for a new assignment.

While I was waiting for my orders, I had a lot of time to think. My jobs consisted of performing guard duty and going out in the field to cut the paratroopers out of the trees when they got caught during a training jump. I also learned how to pack parachutes. I continually wondered where I would be going next. There was so much going on in the world now. Everything had changed since I entered the army a few months earlier.

After six weeks of waiting, I finally received orders for Schweinfurt, Germany. I called home quite often, and I was especially excited to share the good news with my family that I was going to Germany. This was the chance of a lifetime. Hopefully I would have opportunities while I was stationed in Germany to see the rest of Europe as well, and I was very excited about that.

I arrived at the army base at Schweinfurt on December 19, 2001, just six days before Christmas. I have to admit the feelings of loneliness crept in whenever I would let them. Along with the other new troops coming in, I waited at Reception for a bus to pick us up and take us to our unit. There were ten of us altogether, and I didn't know a soul. After I settled into my room, I went out with one of the first guys I met, Kyle Nygaard, who ended up being the best man at my wedding. We went to a bar down the road and just hung out.

It didn't take long for me to get a feel for army life in another country and get into a routine. After I was there for a month, we had our first field problem that consisted of two weeks of training away from the base, secluded in our own world.

My MOS, my job, was artillery. I learned what powders to use, what rounds to use, and what fuses to put on the rounds. We were taught how to use Howitzers, the moving guns. They are big and powerful mechanized artillery you would never want to have anyone pointing at you. Each platoon had three Howitzers and three Cats (the ammo and powder transporter for the Howitzer).

There was an average of 22 to 25 guys in my platoon, the Red Platoon. Four hundred soldiers in all would deploy for a field problem. My entire battalion was the 1st Battalion, 7th Field Artillery. When we were in the field, we did not do the usual physical training we would do back at the post. We would get up, eat breakfast, and go to field training. Sometimes it would be hours before we would shoot a single round. If it was foggy, we had to wait until it was safe to shoot. While we were waiting, we would sleep in the Howitzers. We had our full uniforms on, as if in battle.

While a couple of the trainings I went through were in the summer, most of the time it was very cold, but eventually we got used to it. In the field our rations were MREs (Meals Ready to Eat), and each vehicle had its own rations. There was no such thing as taking a shower, and we used baby wipes to stay clean. When it was time to use the bathroom, we went to the woods.

I went through four more training missions after my first two-week training, and they were three to four weeks long. All our training took place in two large farm areas the army leased, Hohenfels and Grafenwoehr. It took us three and a half hours to get there by bus. We would load all our training vehicles and equipment onto a train the night before we were going to leave. I disliked the first few days in the field, but then I would realize I was saving money because I wasn't going out to the clubs in Schweinfurt every night, so then I would feel better about being there. And, I would come to realize, it was always nice to get away from the regular, everyday routine. Everything went very smoothly in the field. There were some little mistakes, but nothing big. I would always be happy toward the end of field training exercise to get back to Schweinfurt.

Going back to Schweinfurt (or "back to the rear," as we called it), was always exciting. We knew we would be going out and having a good time after several weeks in the field. We would unload the vehicles and take them back to the Motor Pool. We would then have to sit in an unnecessarily long formation and hear a lecture from the Battalion and the Battery Commanders about how we shouldn't try to "drink all of Schweinfurt" in one night. As soon as we were dismissed, we would get cleaned up and then go out and try to "drink all of Schweinfurt" in one night!

I left for Kosovo on a peacekeeping mission on May 6, 2002, and stayed there until November 15, 2002. This mission would prevent me from going to my brother Phil's wedding on June 15. I called my mom before the wedding and cried. It was so difficult for me to miss such an important family event. When I knew the wedding reception was over that day and even though it was the middle of the night at home, I called my mother. I couldn't wait any longer to hear every detail about the wedding. I was glad when that day was over because I was hurting emotionally.

My duties in Kosovo included guard duty and patrolling throughout the cities. We experienced quite a bit of interaction with the citizens. They were always willing to give us information about what had been going on around their village or town. We usually had a translator with us, so communication was not a problem. We would patrol back and forth, across the land, from FOB (Forward Operating Base) Bondsteel to FOB Thunder on the Serbian border where we did joint checkpoints with the Russian army. Both camps had showers, running water, Internet access, and telephones. I always had something to look forward to because I knew I would be able to place a telephone call to or email my friends and family back home.

In my spare time, I went to the gym or the movie theater. I would usually see two new releases every week. I also became very good at Playstation and X-Box games, and I played a lot of basketball. I also played cards with my fellow soldiers, and Spades became the game of choice. Work and training were with the same guys in the same unit, and I began to develop friendships with many of my fellow soldiers.

When we finally left our peacekeeping mission, we were once again excited to get back to Schweinfurt. We went out on the town when we got back, and I have to admit, I don't have too many memories of that night.

It wasn't long after my return to Schweinfurt that I went home for three weeks of leave. I got home on December 10, and the party began. I was elated to see my family, and I spent Christmas with them and my close friends. It was a very special time in my life. I had grown so much during my time in the army. When I returned home, I realized some things had not changed, and some things would never be the same. I was a different person now, and for the most part, I was discovering this was a good thing.

I returned to Schweinfurt on January 3, 2003, and I went right back to work. The readjustment to military life was quick and easy. I was very thankful for that. I was glad to see my army buddies. Life took on a bit of a dull routine, and four months later, we went back to the field for another three weeks of field problem training.

After that, we returned to Schweinfurt for three weeks and then went back again to the field for three more weeks. While we were in the field, we were told that we were going to Iraq in February 2004. Prior to being told, we had read in the Stars and Stripes newspaper that the First Infantry Division was expected to go, so we weren't surprised. When our commander brought our battery together to tell us, we were excited. Everyone was ready to put into use all that we had learned in field training.

I met Katrin in April after I received orders for Iraq. We met at Tabasco's, a local club for the younger generation. She didn't speak English, and I didn't speak German. We started hanging out together and having conversations with the help of a German/English dictionary. She was a lot of fun, and I felt an almost instant attraction to her. The one feature about her that stood out the most was her beautiful smile. We would go to the Schweinfurt public swimming pool and out for dinner. We would watch CNN and MTV on television at Katrin's house. These were the only two stations she received that were broadcast in English. The more we were together, the better my

German got, but Katrin learned my language a lot faster than I learned hers. Communication between us flowed, and we fell in love.

From the time we received the news we were going to Iraq to the day we left once again for field training on October 1, none of us gave much thought to going to war. We went to Hohenfels again and trained for 30 days. We returned to Schweinfurt on November 1. Shortly thereafter, I asked my parents to spend the Christmas holidays in Germany with Katrin and me. I also asked my mother to be sure to bring my birth certificate with her.

My parents were looking forward to coming to Germany for many reasons. Most of all, they wanted to see me one more time before I left for Iraq. Also, I told them a lot about Katrin. I think they knew, especially after I asked for my birth certificate, I was serious about Katrin, and I was probably going to marry her before I left for Iraq. I never worried this might be the last time I would see my parents. I felt like it was just another send-off for me, something my parents did really well.

I went on leave, and Mom, Dad, Katrin, and I had a great time traveling throughout Europe, taking in the sights in France, Switzerland, Italy, Austria, and Germany. The highlight of our trip was when I proposed to Katrin in Rome in the early morning hours on New Year's Day 2004.

My parents went home on January 10, 2004, and it was difficult for me to say goodbye to them. I knew I was going to miss them. I also knew they would not be there when I married Katrin.

Katrin and I married on January 31, 2004 at the courthouse in Schweinfurt. Katrin's friend, Julia, was her matron of honor. Katrin's friend, Britta, and Britta's husband, Kyle, who was my best man, as well as Katrin's mother and sister, and our dear friends, Victor and Michaela, were at our wedding. My cousin, David Riggs, happened to be in England at the time, so he made the trip to Schweinfurt for the wedding. I was pleased someone from my family would be present to share this happy event with us.

Our ceremony was short but meaningful, and we were all very happy that day. We enjoyed a get-together at our apartment right after the ceremony, and we celebrated. We ended the evening at the Irish Pub.

Katrin and I on our wedding day with our witnesses, Julia Graber and Kyle Nygaard.

For that day, the thoughts about going to Iraq were almost forgotten. In reality, though, my wedding was another day in preparation for my deployment to Iraq. I was getting all my affairs in order. I don't think I was aware of it at the time, but I guess I must have realized deep down inside of me I might not return home from Iraq. There were a lot of legal preparations to make with the army before my deployment, and Katrin and I took care of those together.

On February 11, 2004, my unit left for Kuwait on our way to Iraq. Katrin and I finished packing everything I needed to take with me, and we went to the bus that would take my fellow soldiers and me to the airport. There we all said our goodbyes.

One of the last soldiers to get on the bus was Sergeant First Class Raymond Jones. With an encouraging and confident smile on his face, he told our tearful family members, "I will bring everybody back home." With that, the doors of the bus closed.

I looked out the window at Katrin, blew her a kiss and mouthed the words, "I love you," until I couldn't see her anymore. I laid my head on the back of my seat and stared at the ceiling. I remembered the guardian angel medal my mother had given me that I carried in the front pocket of my pants. I put my hand on the Soldier's Bible in my back pocket my parents had given me during their Christmas visit. Just knowing I had both of these treasures with me made me feel safe. I was embarking on a treacherous journey, and I was scared.

We arrived at the airport for the three-hour flight to Kuwait. I slept most of the time we were in the air. Kuwait was a lot of sand, a ton of heat, and a whole bunch of tents. We took a bus from the airport to Camp New York, the holding area troops go to until they are sent to their base in Iraq. Because it was so hot, our tents had industrial air conditioners in them, and we were able to settle in with some measure of comfort.

We had many conveniences, including a shower about a half-mile away. Unfortunately, by the time you walked back after a shower, you were dirty again from all the blowing sand. The food was pretty good and was served in a mess tent. No cell phones or Internet were available for our use. If you had a phone card, AT& T had a tent set up with a phone available for us to use.

In one of my first phone calls to Katrin from Kuwait, I asked, "How are you?"

She replied, "We are fine."

"What?" I asked.

She said, "Yes, I'm pregnant."

I had no reservations about becoming a dad. In fact, I was really happy with the thought that when I returned from Iraq, I would have my wife and baby waiting for me. And, if I didn't return, I would leave a part of me for Katrin and my parents.

While we were in Kuwait, we trained as we waited to enter Iraq. Our rifle range training was extensive. We practiced shooting 50 cal, MK19, M16, M4, M9, 249 SAW, 240 Bravo, and AT-4 weapons. We learned Close Quarter Marksmanship training – CQM training – how to effectively and safely clear rooms in structures. There were no recreational facilities there, and all we did was train, work, work out, and sleep. We knew we would be there about 22 days before we "crossed the berm," as they called it, into Iraq.

The time finally came for us to travel to Bayji, Iraq, the place where we would be stationed. Two hundred trucks drove up together. Four guys, including me, stayed back to load vehicles. A few days later, we flew to Life Support Area Anaconda, 150 miles south of Bayji. Upon our arrival, we were taken by truck to FOB (Forward Operating Base) Summerall. On the way there, I saw a lot of rundown towns and cities, and people living in poverty. The base was an old Iraqi air force barracks, and it, too, was run down. We had running water for showers, and eventually we had satellite TV, computers for email, and an army landline to make telephone calls. When I called home, I would call Niagara Falls Air Reserve Station, and the operator would connect my phone call to my parent's home.

On the same day we arrived, we went on our first mission. It wasn't long before I realized just how dangerous it was there. The mission was a night patrol on foot through the city. I was simultaneously excited and scared to be in Iraq on patrol. We were out to enforce the 9:00 p.m. curfew in the city. The citizens' houses weren't too bad. They were run down on the outside, but they were decent on the inside. They had electricity and running water, televisions, refrigerators, some had stoves, and some cooked over a fire in a fireplace or a barbeque pit in their backyard. The women wore the traditional Iraqi garb, and the men wore long shirts. The children wore clothing like we see in the U.S. Since this was summertime, many people slept on the roof of their home because they didn't have air conditioning. Most of the people made their living working as farmers, butchers, in retail, oil refineries, and as policemen and Iraqi National Guardsmen. Unfortunately, some Iraqi citizens fed their families with the money they received from killing Americans.

We would get shot at most often on the Market Street, Bayji patrol. One day, while on patrol, I saw a Buffalo Bills sweatshirt for sale in a store, but we were unable to stop. I would have liked to purchase it since the Bills are my hometown football team. It was very strange how I could be thinking about a football team at the same time I was thinking about how I was going to stay alive.

Sometimes we would sit in a field near the mosque and listen to the Imam. We would listen for propaganda against Americans. They broadcasted their morning prayer and message for the whole town to hear. One day, we were on our way to pick up the police, and we saw insurgents with RPGs (rocket propelled grenade launchers) on the roofs of the buildings. They fired at us. Thank God they missed, and our gunner got both of them. I experienced more killing than I want to think about.

This is Barch, one of my fellow soldiers, and I during one of our workouts.

Here is my buddy Scaggs and I with an Iraq citizen.

My buddies Hernandez, Barch, and I in the back row, McClain and Banuelos in front. We had just returned to our post from a patrol.

On April 9, 2004, Good Friday, we suffered our first personnel losses. It was a Muslim holiday, and our platoon was ordered to go to the police station around noon in case there was anti-American protesting. The town was very quiet, and this was a sign to us that something was up. We were sitting in the police station, relaxing, waiting for something to happen. A "dirty cop" (of course no one knew this at that moment) reported to his commander there were some men with RPGs walking to the mayor's office. Originally my squad was supposed to check on the mayor's office situation, but because it was the middle of the day, and the other squad needed some experience, they were sent instead.

Our platoon leader, First Lieutenant Alvery, took the first squad out with First Sergeant Grinston. Within minutes, we saw signal flares, and we heard small arms fire and the sounds of RPGs exploding. We weren't exactly sure where we were going, but we knew we better quickly figure it out. We raced toward the sound of the gunfire to a location about a half-mile away. We heard on the radio three of our men were down. By the time we got there, the adrenalin was racing through our bodies. We ran into the middle of the situation and started picking up our guys who were already dead. We were shooting, screaming, and crying, all at the same time. We put our casualties in the trucks with as much gentleness as we could, considering what was going on around us, and raced out of there. I was sick, and I was stunned. I had just experienced the true reality of war, and I was unable to fully comprehend what I had just seen.

One of the dead was Sergeant First Class Raymond Jones. He would not be able to "bring everybody home" like he told our families he would do when we left Schweinfurt on the bus. I knew that everyone who had been there the day we left Schweinfurt for Iraq would remember Sergeant Jones saying those comforting words to them with confidence in his voice and a smile on his face. They were going to be devastated, just like we were.

The whole event at the mayor's office was a set-up. First Lieutenant Alvery, the squad leader, had only been in Iraq for four days, and he was one of the soldiers who had been injured. I was scared. It could have been me who was killed. Instead, my buddies were dead. My emotions were a flat line for days. We all walked around like robots, reliving the whole scene, knowing we would never forget what we saw happen to our brothers in arms. They were gone forever, never to return to their loved ones who were waiting for them at home with outstretched arms and hope in their hearts.

We were not sent out on another mission for quite a few days. We went through a debriefing. This was a time for us to talk out our feelings. I had seen things that day I had only read about before. It was at this time that my buddies, Barch, McClain, Olds, Whitmeyer, Cirrincione, Scaggs, Hernandez, and I became family. We needed each other now more than ever. We reaffirmed our vow to each other. We would watch each other's backs. We would be there for each other, no matter what.

On July 6, we were waiting at the gate for the Iraqi police to meet us to go on a mission when we heard over the truck radio that our barracks was on fire. We still had to go on our mission, and when we returned an hour later, our rooms were giant ashtrays. I remember my first reaction was to laugh, and before you knew it, we were all laughing. That might sound crazy, but we all still had our lives, and in Iraq, your life was your only possession you were really worried about holding on to. I lost all my personal belongings — my guitar, photos, letters, and clothing. We were grateful we weren't asleep in the barracks when it burned. The fire was caused by an electrical problem. We were moved to small, two-man C-huts. These became our homes. A few days later, we drove back to Anaconda to get new gear.

Missions were held at all times of the day and night. We never knew when we were going to be sent out. Before going out, we would have to put on all our gear. We usually had only a couple minutes to get ready. How could war become everyday life? I'm not sure how it happens, but it did.

Our July 28 mission was a scheduled mission. We left our camp at 11:15 p.m. That day was a repeat of the "same old stuff" from the day before, including a trip to the gym. Four Humvees (my platoon) were going to meet a National Guard patrol coming from the other direction. Our combat patrol was traveling through Bayji when insurgents started shooting RPGs and small arms fire at us. A dud hit the last few trucks in our patrol. I couldn't see where the RPGs were coming from because I was driving.

We got through the city, out of the "kill zone," as we called it, and we set up a perimeter, a large circle, with our vehicles. Two cars were approaching from the city. My chief and I were asked to go question the people in the cars. We were walking toward the cars. When we were about 40 yards away, we yelled at the occupants to get out of the cars. As their guns appeared from inside the cars, they flipped their high beams on to blind us. That's when we started shooting at the windows of the cars, and the gunfire was returned. Someone yelled, "Pirinelli, watch out!" I turned to the left to see if there was an attack coming from the other direction.

One second after I turned, I felt like someone hit me in the back with a sledgehammer. I turned back around, and I kept shooting. I screamed to my chief I had been hit, but I didn't know what I had been hit with. I didn't realize at first that I had been shot by enemy gunfire. It was only when I looked down and saw my insides hanging out of me that I knew how bad it was. I started to panic and scream.

I fell to the ground, and Chief Banuelos lay on top of me. Amidst all the gunfire and noise, as he was trying to protect himself and me, he kept shouting to me that 80% of gut shots live. He was trying to console me in the middle of a heated battle with the enemy. The shooting got worse. The bullets were hitting all around us. Chief Banuelos was curled up in a ball, half of him next to me and the other half on top of me. It's a wonder he didn't get shot, too. Then the platoon sergeant, Sergeant First Class Ireland, ran over to us. Everyone started yelling that I had been hit, screaming for the truck and the stretcher to pick me up.

In the instant before I began going in and out of consciousness, my heavenly Father, whom I have known since I was a young boy, sent me the peace that passeth all understanding. No matter what happened to me now, I knew God was with me. As I lay there on my back, I could feel my Soldier's Bible in my back pocket, and I remembered my guardian angel medal in my front pocket. They both reminded me that God would take care of me. As scared as I was and with all the scattered thoughts racing through my mind, I knew, one way or another, no matter what the outcome, I would be okay. I had no doubt God was reassuring me. "John, you can consider it done."

CLINGING TO THE WINGS
OF AN ANGEL

by Ruth

☆ ☆ ☆

John is my nephew, and one of the precious branches of our family tree. When I think of our family tree, a vivid picture enters my mind. I am reminded of the redwoods in the Sierras of California that I admired during the years California was my home. I left my wonderful family and Western New York in 1970 with my husband to make a home with his family in Stockton, California. I missed my mom and dad, my sister Risë, and my brother Roy, but during those years we lived so far apart, our family tree continued to grow tall and strong. I had two daughters, Risë (Little Risë, as the family fondly calls her) and Kristy. Even though I lived 3,000 miles away, I was Aunt Ruthie and was very close to my six nephews, Robby, Philip and John (my sister's boys) and Tim, Michael and Jeffrey (my brother's boys). We enjoyed great fun during my yearly visits. In 1984, my husband and I divorced, and I moved back to Western New York with my girls. With our move, the family tree's branches were not spread as far. Eventually I would marry my sister's husband's brother, Lou Pirinelli, and we would have our daughter, Dawn. The family tree continued to grow. Just as my girls became like daughters to my brother and sister, my nephews became like sons to me. We felt so blessed to have each other.

The redwood tree has a vast root system, a huge trunk with thick bark, and many, many branches with cones on the tips of the upper branches. It lives for centuries. Because the root system of these trees is surprisingly shallow, often going down only three to six feet, the trees depend on balance to remain standing. The redwood grows in a stunning forest among other species of trees and wildlife in an incredible place only God, the great Creator, could have fashioned.

Our family is like a giant redwood tree. Our parents are the roots. The trunk, with its thick bark that protects it, is their three children. The branches are their grandchildren, and the cones on the top branches are their great-grandchildren. Without a doubt, our family has become stronger, taller and sturdier with the passage of time. Our children have been fortunate to grow up in a beautiful forest of loving and caring people. The delicate cones on the tips of the upper branches represent the children of the most recent generation that have just started coming along in the last few years. They are treasured the most. Our family tree depends on the balance a loyal and loving family brings to each of us. The family grows and is nourished in a forest of love also created by God.

However, fire or a fierce coastal storm can blast through the forest and upset not only the trees but also every living thing around the trees. There have been some serious storms in our family, and our roots have been tugged at and sometimes exposed, but our family tree has not been uprooted. On June 26, 1988, my father, Edwin Klein, and the root of our beautiful redwood tree, entered the hospital for colon cancer surgery. While he was in surgery, we went to the chapel at the hospital to pray for his quick and complete recovery. We put him in God's hands, and we were elated when his surgeon delivered the news to us that Dad's surgery was a complete success. The doctor was able to remove the cancerous tumor, and we were thankful Dad would have a complete recovery. Needless to say, we were overjoyed. And so, just like we did for any other member of our family who was ill or in the hospital, we showered him with love and attention. He was in pain, but he was a strong and young-for-his-age 74-year-old man we all adored. He had his faith in God to bring him through this tough time, just like his faith had brought him through other difficulties throughout his life.

On the morning of June 30, 1988, we received a telephone call from one of Dad's nurses that Dad's blood sugar had dropped to a dangerous low of 20, and we should come to the hospital. He was suffering. He was sweating and shaking and sometimes incoherent, but not enough to keep him from wondering what was wrong. We kept reassuring him he would be okay, and that the doctors knew what they were doing. He received bolus after bolus of glucose and glasses of orange juice. In spite of various treatments to elevate his blood sugar, nothing seemed to be working. After hours of attempts to raise his blood sugar, he was moved to the hospital's Intensive Care Unit. At 10:00 p.m. that night, he died.

After much time passed and other cases of unexplained low blood sugar (hypoglycemia) occurred at the same hospital, a certain nurse was arrested, tried, and convicted of criminally negligent homicide for intentionally overdosing Dad and other patients on insulin, but in all these cases, Dad was the only one who died from her mistreatment. She is still in prison serving her sentence of at least 11-1/3 years.

One might wonder how a family could ever stick together and come even closer to God after such a traumatic event. It wasn't always easy, but the thought we consistently held onto was that Dad was a Christian man, and we knew he was in heaven.

To finally reveal what happened to Dad was not an easy task. It took seven years of investigating, including the exhumation of Dad's body three years after he died, six amendments to his death certificate, and the dedication of a courageous public official, Niagara County Coroner James Joyce, to bring closure to this terrible event. In the end, after a long and tiresome struggle, including the nurse's criminal trial, justice was served. Our family tree withstood the storm, and its roots remained firmly planted.

A person might wonder what all this has to do with John. I will explain. When you have been through such a traumatic event, you have two choices. You can become angry with God, pushing Him away, or you can heal your wounds in the comfort of His loving arms and open your eyes to the power He has. We chose the latter, and He was so good to us. Even though Dad was not with us on earth anymore, God gave us the strength and the wisdom to lead the fight to stop this nurse from ever hurting anyone else again. The wonderful people we met who were so willing to fight for our cause will remain lifelong friends. We saw the power of God as He provided every bit of strength and knowledge needed by our family to get us through this ordeal and to realize justice when it was over.

People would often say to us after the nurse was convicted that Dad could now rest in peace, but we knew Dad had been resting in peace since the moment he died. What we came to realize was that now we could live in peace with his death. So, when John was so severely injured and hanging onto his life by a thread, we knew just what to do. After all, we had been through the drill before. Faith and prayer would bring us through.

As our family redwood tree became more mature, some of us moved to other parts of the tree. Some of us became part of the roots, some of us became part of the trunk, and others remained the branches. It evolves on its own over time, just like the world keeps spinning. Strengths and weaknesses place us in the appropriate part of the tree. My position on the tree was the trunk, the area of the tree through which the food from the roots flows. You can't have a tree without a trunk. Those of us in the family who make up the trunk are the go-to people of the family, the people who keep the branches growing and thriving in the magnificent forest of life. So, it wasn't any surprise to me when I was asked to do what appeared to be the impossible on Sunday, August 1, 2004.

With the news of John's injury and critical condition, Philip and Stephanie desperately wanted to be by John's side. The Sunday morning we received word from the army that John had taken a turn for the worse, Philip was terrified. Amidst the relatives who were still at his home after the cousins' weekend reunion, Phil ran to the back deck of his house and cried out in agony and fear that his dear brother was going to die. There wasn't one thing anyone could do to comfort him, not even Stephanie. At that point, all any of us could do was get dressed and go to church.

Risë and Bob had already gone to the first service. It was almost over when the rest of us started arriving at our church, St. Matthew Lutheran Church in North Tonawanda, New York. The only comfort to be received on that day and for many, many days thereafter was going to come from God. As far as our family was concerned, the only human being all of us knew and trusted on earth who could bring us as close as possible to God was our dear Pastor Moldenhauer. With these overwhelming feelings of dread and anxiety, Pastor prepared a private communion table for us. There we were, some in our shorts and tee shirts, receiving the body and the blood of Jesus Christ. Our prayers were disjointed. We knew we should first begin our prayers by asking God to forgive us for all our sins, but, for most of us, our pleas to our heavenly Father to save John overtook us. I'm sure the Lord understood. With our pastor's consoling prayers came the gentle but firm reminder that if it was God's will John should go to heaven now, then that is what would happen, and we all must accept God's will. Pastor asked God to put his loving arms around John and heal his body. Pastor also asked God to bring peace and quiet confidence to all of us as we were reminded He is in charge, and, from the day each of us was born, He has always had a perfect plan for our lives.

When communion was over and the prayers in church were finished, we all left with our heads bowed. Yes, we had to believe God. We had to trust Him. We hadn't spent all these years worshipping and professing to be Christians to now abandon everything we had been taught, just at the moment when we may need it more than we ever had in our lives. We had learned so much through our previous trials and tribulations. We just couldn't throw it all away. No, we were going to believe, we were going to ask God for a miracle, and we were going to do it unceasingly.

We all gathered at Risë and Bob's home after church and began to make the plans that would take John's parents to his bedside in Germany. Sergeant Bowman from the Casualty Division of the Army called, and she and I finalized the arrangements with the airlines for Risë and Bob to go to Germany the next day. Thank God, Risë and Bob had gotten their passports when they went to Germany to visit John and Katrin before John went to Iraq. Philip and

Stephanie didn't have passports, and we all knew it took a minimum of three weeks to get passports. Philip, 6'6", dark-haired and handsome, was pacing back and forth, driven by worry about his brother and his parents. He was also thinking about how he could get himself and his wife to Germany. It would take a miracle. He knew that. Finally he sat down at the table across from me. He looked me straight in the eye and, with desperation, asked me if I could think of any way we might be able to make this happen. "Aunt Ruth, I need to be with John. I need to tell him to get up out of his bed. He is a warrior. He is a survivor. He needs to fight. If I can just be with him, I can give him the strength he needs. I can talk to him, and I know he will hear me."

This was all he had to say to me. I would do anything to bring these two brothers, my dear nephews, together. The wheels in my head started turning. When a "go-to" person is faced with a challenge, there is no rest until the challenge has been conquered. It warms my heart to know that Philip knew if he asked me, and I couldn't do it, then it couldn't be done. At that moment, he placed on me one of the biggest burdens I would ever carry in my life. I was up for it, and I thank God now I would only carry it for a few hours.

I went into one of the bedrooms at Risë and Bob's house to think. Shortly thereafter, Stephanie joined me. We sat on the bed next to each other, and I told her we needed to pray. "Dear Lord, you know our hearts. You know, Lord, at this moment, Philip and Stephanie desperately want to go to Germany to be with John and to provide support for Risë and Bob. Lord, I don't even know where to begin to help them. Please give me wisdom and perseverance as I try to figure this out. If it is your will for Philip and Stephanie to go to Germany, then it will be done. And, Lord, I will be honored and proud to be your servant."

I went to the closet to get the telephone book. Politicians can be helpful in a case like this. But, it was Sunday afternoon. Even politicians deserve a day off. I decided I would try anyway. I called U.S. Senator Hillary Clinton's office and left a message. "Who knows," I thought. "Maybe the staffers check the messages on Sunday." I called U.S. Senator Charles Schumer's office and left a message there as well. I called the office of Assemblywoman Francine DelMonte. No answer there, either. I called the Red Cross, and I did talk with a very nice gentleman there, but he told me the Red Cross would not be able to help with getting passports. That was strictly a function of the federal government. He gave me the telephone number of the Southern Tier Military Parents Support Group, who would later become our dear friends and supporters, but I was unable to talk to anyone on Sunday. Again I left a message.

Finally, as I cried out to God again for help, I thought of New York State Senator George Maziarz. He is known for his kindness and patriotism. I went to the residential listings in the telephone book, and lo, and behold, there was his home telephone number. I dialed the number, and he answered. It was 2:25 p.m.

"Senator Maziarz, my name is Ruth Pirinelli, and I need your help."

"How can I help you?" he asked.

"My nephew, John Pirinelli, is in the army. He was shot in Iraq on Thursday. He is now in Germany at Landstuhl Regional Medical Center in critical condition. His parents will be leaving tomorrow afternoon for Germany. John's brother, Philip, and his wife, Stephanie, want to go as well, but they don't have passports. Can you help?"

"Let me make a few telephone calls. I am going to give you my cell phone number. Stay by the phone. I will call you back."

I hung up the phone. I was absolutely stunned the senator answered the phone. But then I thought of Romans 8:28. "And we know that all that happens to us is working for our good if we love God and are fitting into his plans." I would find out later that the senator had been home for 20 minutes that day, just to pick something up, and was on his way out the door to go to back to Albany when he heard his telephone ringing. Thank God he answered it!

The first call the senator made was to Cathy Clement. In the past, she worked with the senator at the Niagara County Clerk's Office. She knows everything there is to know about passports. Cathy told him there was a passport office in New York City. She also offered to download the applications, help Phil and Steph fill them out and then check their paperwork to make sure they had everything they needed.

The senator also called Congressman Tom Reynolds regarding the New York City passport office. The Congressman gave Senator Maziarz all the pertinent information needed as to where the office was and what time it opened.

With that, Senator Maziarz called me back.

"Hello, Ruth, this is George. There is a passport office in New York City. Philip and Stephanie will be able to get their passports there tomorrow morning. They will have to be there by 5:30 a.m. to get in line. I will take them there."

"You will do what?" I asked the senator, certain I heard him wrong.

"I will drive them. I will pick up my aide, Mike Norris, in Albany who is familiar with New York City, and we will get them to the passport office early in the morning."

"Senator, I don't know what to say."

"You don't have to say anything. The only documents Philip and Stephanie will need are their driver's licenses, their social security cards and their birth certificates. They should go home now and get packed. I will meet you at my office in two hours. A very good friend of mine from the Clerk's Office will meet us there and help them fill out the applications and make sure all their paperwork is in order."

Now, I am usually not a person of few words, but all I could say was, "Thank you, Senator, and God bless you."

"I am glad to help," the senator said, and with that, we hung up.

I ran to find Phil and Steph and tell them what the senator had said. In my excitement, I could hardly get it out.

For the first time since Thursday, I saw a smile on both of their faces. There was hope. There is always hope, and this proved it! We firmed up the tentative airline reservations they made, and off they went, practically running, going home to get the documents they needed. They would throw some clothes into a suitcase and be right back.

Everyone at the house was jubilant. What we thought was "the impossible" had been done. Praise the Lord! This was the shot in the arm that everyone needed.

About a half hour later, in the midst of all the excitement, I almost didn't hear the phone ringing. I answered with a happy, "Hello!"

It was Stephanie. "Aunt Ruth, we have been searching for our birth certificates, and all of a sudden it came to us. We don't have them. The social worker took them when we applied for the adoption of a baby."

Philip and Stephanie can't have children of their own. When Stephanie was eight years old, she had cancer. Her reproductive organs were destroyed during her cancer treatments. When Philip met pretty and petite Stephanie with her long, blonde hair, she told him she couldn't have children, but that didn't matter to Philip. He had fallen in love with this pretty nurse. He wanted her to be his wife. "We'll just adopt our children," Philip would say. "There are a lot of kids out there who need a home, and we will open ours to them."

I told Steph, "Don't panic. I will call Senator Maziarz and tell him. We have come so far. I cannot believe you two are not going to Germany tomorrow."

I called the senator on his cell phone. "Senator, this is Ruth again. We have a roadblock. Phil and Steph's birth certificates are in the Erie County Surrogate Court. They have applied for an adoption. What are we going to do?"

"Ruth, stay calm. Give me a few minutes. I will get back to you."

Senator Maziarz called State Supreme Court Justice Richard Kloch at home, interrupting a family barbecue, and asking for help. Judge Kloch reached Mr. Paul Smaldone, the clerk to Surrogate Judge Barbara Howe. Mr. Smaldone interrupted a family outing to contact Judge Howe to get permission to go into the courthouse and get the birth certificates out of the file.

Judge Howe quickly gave her permission, and Mr. Smaldone and another clerk went to the courthouse and found the birth certificates. It sounded to me like he would be looking for a needle in a haystack, but when something is God's plan, all things are possible. At 7:00 p.m., the senator met Mr. Smaldone and picked up the birth certificates.

Senator Maziarz called me regularly with updates as to how the search for the birth certificates was progressing, and his final telephone call to me was, "Ruth, I have the birth certificates. Bring Phil and Steph to my office at 8:30 p.m. Cathy Clement will meet us there to check the passport paperwork, and then we will be on the road to Albany to pick up Mike Norris, my assistant. We will arrive in New York City early in the morning."

By this time, Phil and Steph had returned to Risë and Bob's house. Those poor kids were on pins and needles with each turn of events. The house was full of people watching this drama unfold, and at 8:00 p.m., when the three of us left for the senator's office, we were all shedding tears of joy for the first time in days. We had experienced God. We had just seen a miracle.

At 9:00 p.m., after making sure all the paperwork was in order, Senator Maziarz, Phil and Steph pulled out of the parking lot at the senator's office, just six and a half hours after I first called the senator. I stood there in amazement. They were going to make it to Germany. "God, You heard our pleas, and You made it happen," I prayed silently. How awesome it is to experience God's power.

As the senator, Phil and Steph made their way down the New York State Thruway, they talked about everything from politics to religion. A few months later, the senator affectionately remarked he was sure he had heard Phil's opinion on just about every subject you could think of. They took turns driving. They listened to the radio, and they took turns trying to sleep. Then they heard reports of terrorist threats directed at the New York Stock Exchange in New York. Needless to say, this news made them very uneasy.

At 2:30 a.m., they arrived in Albany and picked up the senator's staffer, Mike Norris. At 5:00 a.m., the weary travelers crossed the George Washington

Bridge en route to lower Manhattan, right into the financial district that was on high alert because of the terrorist threats. Stephanie was nervous about traveling over the bridge because of the terrorist threats, but she knew in her heart God did not bring them this far to let anything happen to them. At 5:30 a.m., Monday, August 2, 2004, they arrived at the passport office and were third in line.

By 11:00 a.m., Phil and Steph had their passports in hand and had arrived at LaGuardia Airport in plenty of time for their 4:00 p.m. flight to Germany. Still running on adrenalin, their parting words to the senator were, "When John comes home we'll all get together for a big barbecue. Thanks so much." The senator thought the suggestion of a barbecue was appropriate since everyone he had asked to help the day before had interrupted their barbecues to so willingly do their part for a family in distress.

Finally, Phil and Steph could relax for a while until it was time to begin the final leg of their journey that would take them to John. Stephanie called us from the airport to let us know the mission had been accomplished and they were ready to go. I asked to speak to Phil. In his exhaustion he laid down on the cold, hard airport floor and was fast asleep.

When I arrived home on Monday afternoon, after taking Bob and Risë to the airport, I sat at my kitchen table and pondered all the events of the last few days. I wondered how I would ever be able to sufficiently thank all the compassionate Americans who had been there for us, with heart and soul, to help a wounded soldier and his family in any way they could. With all the pressures and time constraints public officials live with, I was astonished at everything Senator Maziarz had accomplished in a few hours. I thought people should know what he had done for us. I called a local television station and told them I thought I had a great story to tell about a caring politician and loyal American. Within a few hours, the word had spread, and all three local TV stations were parked in front of Risë and Bob's house with their reporters on stand-by and broadcasting equipment ready to go.

This was a story of Americans helping Americans. This was the kind of positive story people needed to hear as opinions on the war in Iraq divided families and demolished lifetime friendships. Watching footage of the war on TV and reading accounts in the newspaper of the toll being taken on our troops and their families was, to say the least, overwhelming for most Americans.

The interviews I did that night with the reporters would mark the beginning of my new role as the family spokesperson. People were not only intrigued with the news about what Senator Maziarz had done for our family, they were clamoring for news about John. The two stories went hand in hand. "NYS Senator helps family of wounded soldier," "Maziarz goes extra mile to get passports," "Maziarz: A man for all reasons," "Brother makes it to wounded soldier's side, with a little help." My personal favorite was entitled, "Wounded soldier's recovery seen as uncanny development; Maziarz lauded for help." This story portrayed the miracle that John was still alive, and the miracle of how one politician was able to bring to John's bedside what his doctors called "his best medicine" — his family.

John was still alive, and his family members were on their way to give him the strength and determination he would need as he fought for his life. Our family tree had survived yet another storm.

Once again, God spoke to us through His miracles. "Trust in me. I sent an angel to you today. Hold onto his wings. He will take you where you need to go. Your prayers will be answered. You can consider it done."

THE PRAYER CHAIN GROWS

by Ruth

☆ ☆ ☆

As I watched my sister, Risë, and my brother-in-law, Bob, walk down the corridor toward the gate at the Buffalo/Niagara International Airport, beginning their journey to their injured son's bedside in Germany, my heart ached for them. I realized how brave and faithful my sister and her husband are. It was obvious to me that John had come by his bravery very naturally. They "just knew" John was going to be all right. They were experiencing alternating moments of tears and then peace. Even though John's doctors were not overly encouraging about his condition during the telephone conversations Bob and Risë had with them, the doctors still wanted them to have hope John could recover from his injuries.

They had experienced the miracle of Philip and Stephanie getting their passports. Recalling this miraculous event gave them the courage they needed to face the future.

As I lost sight of them, I turned around and paused for a minute. I couldn't even see where I was going; my eyes were so filled with tears of grief. I was so scared. I felt so tired and completely worn out. The last few days, with all the ups and downs and happiness and sadness we'd endured, had taken their toll on me. The only reason I kept going was because I saw the power of God so clearly and so often. In the last few days He had brought all of us so much happiness and sometimes even delight during those dark hours and days.

When I finally arrived home, I couldn't remember driving there. Risë and Bob, on their flight from Buffalo, and Phil and Stephanie, on their flight from New York City, would get to Germany about the same time. All of us would be so thankful when John wasn't alone anymore, but then we realized John had never been alone. We had been praying for a guardian angel to be with him since he went into the army, and his angel was doing a miraculous job!

My telephone was ringing and ringing. Sometimes my cell phone and my home phone were ringing at the same time. My cousin, Janet, called me to see how everything was going. "Everything is okay. A lot of good things happened this weekend, and for that I am eternally grateful. My problem now is I don't know how I am going to do everything I have to do for Risë, Bob, Philip, and Stephanie, and still go to work, keep my life going, and keep all these wonderful people who are calling informed about John's condition." In addition, since the news about John being wounded had hit the media, I was receiving telephone calls from the television, news-paper, and radio stations asking for news on John's condition. The TV reporters told me their viewers were calling them, clamoring for information about John. Complete strangers had already adopted John. Some say people just don't care anymore. I will never believe that statement ever again in my life.

I was collecting email addresses for an address book just for "John Updates." I was relieved when my cousin, Janet, who is one of the most giving and kind people I have ever known, offered to take over the email addresses, organize the address book, and send out the daily updates on John. Another prayer was answered! Janet's first email went out on Tuesday, August 3, 2004. When God empowers you, there is no mountain you can't climb! Janet proved that when she took on a huge and time-consuming job. The email list started with 20 addresses, and it quickly grew to at least 75. It would continue to grow during the following months to include hundreds.

Risë and Bob arrived in Detroit for a short layover before their non-stop flight to Frankfurt, Germany. They called me just to be sure there wasn't any news about John. They had only been out of touch for an hour and a half, but even that was too long with their son's life dangling on a very thin thread. I was happy to tell them I had not heard anything from John's doctors, so no news was good news. I wished them well on their long trip across the Atlantic, and I could sense the excitement in their voices. Risë had been saying from the moment she found out John was injured that she could not bear the thought of him being there without his family. She just wanted to be by his bedside and hold his hand and comfort him. She tried to put out of her mind how much pain he probably was in, but that was a difficult thing for a mother to do. I kept reminding her that God and his angels were right there with John. "Of course," she said, "I know. That thought is what I will hold onto."

We had to end our conversation as it was time for them to board the plane that would take them to John's beside. "I love you," I said. "Everything is going to be all right." I hoped I had convinced them, because I was still very, very scared.

After Risë and Bob arrived in Germany, Risë called me to let me know they were there. She couldn't wait to share a story with me about something that happened during their flight. There was a group of young people and their pastor on the plane, traveling to Kenya to do missionary work, and Risë heard them talking. She asked the pastor if she could talk to him for a moment. He readily agreed, and she told him about John and why they were going to Germany. Within minutes, the pastor gathered all of his young people, the surrounding passengers, and the flight attendants together, and they began to pray for John. She recalled almost every word of the prayer he said. "Lord, we don't know John, but we know You do. Lord, he is hurting, he is severely injured, and he might die. Lord, if it is Your will to have John come to heaven with You now, we will respect that. But, Dear Lord, please, put Your loving and healing arms around John; heal his wounds, Lord, and please, if it is Your will, grant our wish and allow him to remain on earth with his loving family for a very long time. He is a brave man, and he has given a lot to his country, Lord. We love him for that. And we would ask for your continuous healing of John, in the name of Jesus Christ, our Lord and Savior, Amen."

She told me that when all the bowed heads raised and she looked around, she saw eyes full of tears. She realized that our troops don't just belong to one family, one unit, one branch of the military, or one command. All Americans love them. Risë and Bob's burden was being shared, and what a comfort that was to them.

Risë then told me another story about the kindness they experienced during their flight. A gentleman and his nephew sitting next to Bob and Risë on the flight started talking with them. They were going to a wedding in Lithuania, and they, too, wanted to pray for John. Once again, Bob and Risë prayed for John with people that wouldn't know John if John walked right up to them. When their prayers were finished, one of the gentlemen told Bob and Risë John's story would be part of the liturgy he would be delivering at his son's wedding the next day. The attendees at the wedding of someone that lives in a foreign country would be praying for their son! Risë remarked that only God could make wedding plans like that!

She reported that the rest of their flight to Germany was peaceful. They were grateful when they arrived in Frankfurt to see that Philip and Stephanie had also arrived safely. Army officials who were taking them to see John were waiting for them when they got off the plane. Risë also told me she noticed their respectful stature as they stood at attention. I thanked God once again that Risë, Bob, Philip and Stephanie had all arrived safely in Germany.

The next day brought some relief for me from all the tension, thinking about my loved ones and John, and asking God once again to keep them safe and in His care. I knew God heard me the first time I asked Him, but I prayed unceasingly because that is what God tells us to do. My daughter, Kristy, called me to see how I was. "I am exhausted, but I'm okay."

"Mom, what do you think about having a prayer vigil for John and for all the troops?"

"Kristy, there is no way I have the strength or energy to plan an event like a prayer vigil. Besides, we would have to have it really soon, and I don't see how we could pull it together. If you want to take over, I will help you."

"Yes, Mom, that's what I want to do. Michelle Foster has offered to help. She has known John for a long time, and she wants to do something to help him. We are going to get started."

"Okay, honey, just let me know what is going on and what you need. I think you better call Pastor first and see when he is available and then plan from there."

And, so, that is what Kristy did. She called Pastor. He thought a prayer vigil was a great idea. "Yes," he would be available on Thursday, August 5. That was just three days away. How in the world would we pull this together? "All things are possible through Christ, the Lord, who strengthens me." This Bible verse kept reverberating through my mind. After all the miracles I had seen so far, I was thinking another one would make this prayer vigil a reality.

The next call Kristy made was to the City of North Tonawanda Mayor's Office to see if Gateway Park was available. Gateway Park is a beautiful marina nestled on the banks of the Erie Canal. It was the perfect place to hold an event like this. It was the first place she thought of because right after the September 11 terrorist attacks on America, our family went to a prayer vigil at this same location, and it was an inspirational night none of us will ever forgot.

"Yes," Gateway Park was available. Now it was time to get down to the details. All I can say is, with very little effort on our part, everything kept falling into place. I was the mistress of ceremonies, so to speak, and our pastor, Rev. A. W. Moldenhauer, led us in prayer. The city provided a gentleman who operated the sound system at Gateway Park for us.

We asked Linda Robinson, a woman we knew from church, if she could lead us in song. Linda has a beautiful voice and sings at our church quite often. "Yes," she was available and was honored to be part of the program.

We wondered if Senator Maziarz would be available so he could say a few words about the miracles he had seen in the past few days and how he was part of the one that led to Phil and Stephanie getting their passports so they could go to Germany to be with John. "Yes," he was very happy to attend and was more than willing to say a few words.

An event praying for the military and John needed to be advertised because our prayers were going to be for all our soldiers, not just for John. I contacted the TV stations, and, of course, they told me they would be very happy to advertise the prayer vigil being held not only for John but also for all the troops. We knew a lot of area people who had loved ones in the military who would welcome the chance to join in prayer for their soldier and for all the troops.

We needed a color guard. There are several men at our church who oftentimes presented the colors. We called them and the Niagara Falls Air Reserve Station, and before we knew it, we had a full color guard of men and women, representing the various branches of the military. They told us they would be honored to take part in the program. Their presence in full uniform reminded everyone at the prayer vigil that our troops deserve our utmost respect and need our unending support for all the sacrifices they make for all of us so that we can all enjoy freedom.

Our pastor suggested we should have a program that included the words to all the songs we were going to sing as well as the order of the hour-long service. I do this type of work in the course of my regular job duties, and I could do the layout, but the cost of printing would have been very expensive. My daughter's employer, Ivoclar Vivadent, Inc. in Amherst, wanted to do something to help. When she asked the vice president of the company if he could arrange for the printing, he said the company would be honored to help in any way it could to make the prayer vigil a success. Ivoclar Vivadent, Inc. generously covered the printing costs.

Such an important event had to be memorial-ized on videotape. I didn't know whom I could ask to do that because all our family members wanted to take part in the prayer vigil. I called a good friend I work with, Debbie Heim. She asked her son, Steven, if he would be available to do the videotaping. "Of course," he said, he would be honored to help in any way he could.

A sunset prayer vigil had to have candlelight. Where were we going to get 500 candles? Kristy and Michelle called Life Resources, a local Christian bookstore. They were very happy to donate the candles. They expressed their happiness that they were able to help John and his family.

We really wanted to have a brand new flag we could give to John after the prayer vigil. From time to time, I had purchased flags for my employer from Ace Flag in Buffalo. I called Ace and asked if the company would donate a flag for the prayer vigil. "Of course," they were happy to have one of their flags flying at a prayer vigil for our troops.

We had everything we needed, and we still had some time left. Yes, we had seen another miracle. Our prayer vigil would be held at a beautiful and peaceful setting that could accommodate up to 1,000 people; our wonderful pastor that we love, who can pray like no one we've ever heard, would be our spiritual leader; Linda Robinson who sings like an angel, would inspire our singing voices; our hearts would burst with patriotism as we watched a real military color guard present a brand new flag; and all those who came to pray would follow along with a professionally printed program. They wouldn't miss a precious moment of this event. To top it all off, Cousin Janet made a trip to the music store at the last minute and purchased accompanying music for three of the four hymns we sang. Our music would sound even more beautiful than if we sang acapella.

"Oh, and one last thing, Lord, because this has been one of the rainiest summers we have had in a long time, we are praying for a dry evening. We know we have asked You for a lot these last few days. We pray You will grant us this request. Amen."

Once again, we saw God at work in our preparations. The one arrangement for the prayer vigil that amazed us the most was our speaker from the military, Lieutenant Colonel Hugh Van Roosen. In Kristy's telephone conversations with the personnel at the air base, she tried to find someone who could come to the prayer vigil and say a few words about life in the military, especially during this time of war. Her request had been given to LTC VanRoosen. "Yes," he was happy to be part of the prayer vigil. He would share his incredible story about how he and his unit had recently returned from Iraq where they had defended the same ground John and his unit had. If anyone had any doubt about whether or not God was helping us bring the details of this prayer vigil together, this would have convinced them God was overseeing all the arrangements. These two soldiers had been on the same soil in service to their country. Only God could have brought LTC Van Roosen and our family together on such short notice!

We were so excited. We just knew this would be an event we would be proud of. It was going to be an inspiration to everyone present, and it would bolster spirits, faith, and patriotism. We couldn't wait.

Finally the day we had been waiting for arrived. It was Thursday, August 5, and the sun was shining. It seemed like we had been planning for weeks, but we knew it had only been three days. It is miraculous how much human beings can accomplish when God is on the planning committee.

There were many reasons to be thankful that day. Even though John was still unconscious, he was holding his own. The sun was shining, and there was no rain predicted for the entire day and evening. The word had gotten out about the prayer vigil, and we were expecting at least 200 people to attend. The programs were done, the candles were ready, and the flag would be flying. At 6:00 p.m., we went to the park to make sure everything was set up and ready.

Earlier in the day Risë had faxed to me a letter that she and Bob had received from John's Battalion Commander in Iraq, Lieutenant Colonel Kyle M. McClelland, United States Army, Commanding. She and Bob were so proud of what it said about John, and they wanted me to share it with others. I took it with me to the prayer vigil. It read in part: "The First Lightning family wants to let you know that we truly miss John and that he is constantly in our prayers and thoughts. On the night of 28 July 2004, your son's platoon provided an escort for a logistical patrol from another task force that was passing through the city of Bayji. This patrol came under attack, but escaped without casualties due to the rapid response of John's platoon. In the course of the firefight your son was wounded in the abdomen. He displayed incredible courage in the face of danger and is an example of strength for our entire task force. You may rest assured that he personally contributed to the wounding of two insurgents and ultimately the capture of four anti-coalition forces that will no longer be able to attack U.S. soldiers. John stood out among his fellow soldiers and garnered the respect and admiration of his entire chain of command. He is a husband, father, son, and soldier of unquestionable character. His sacrifice for the security of Iraqi citizens will not be in vain. Each day our sector is becoming safer as we conduct combat patrols, detain insurgents, contribute to the construction of key infrastructure, and protect the foundation of a blossoming democracy. Every member of this task force appreciates the sacrifice of your son and hopes and prays for a speedy recovery. I want to take this opportunity to say thank you for the sacrifices you have made to the 'First Lightning' task force. John will always be part of our family and I will ensure that we will remain in contact with you and John through correspondence, phone calls, and emails as he recovers." Underneath his typed signature, LTC McClelland wrote, "My thoughts and prayers continue; the team is with you all!!" John's condition had begun to stabilize, and this message about John expressed in the words of this letter were more than a family could ask for. We were speech-less. John was, without a doubt, an American Hero. I shared the letter that night with many people.

Janet arrived with her music CDs, and we had a dress rehearsal with the sound system. The sounds of *Amazing Grace, God Bless America,* and *Let There Be Peace on Earth* resounded throughout the downtown area of North Tonawanda and out across the waters behind the podium. They were the sounds of love and patriotism, just what so many Americans need these days.

Then the people started to arrive. It was a beautiful night, and we were finishing the final preparations. My cell phone was ringing. It was Risë calling me from Germany. She wanted me to describe the evening in detail — the weather, the flowers, the flags, and the people. She was so happy to be with John, but I knew that if she could have somehow magically appeared here just for this one hour, she would have left John to come here to pray with hundreds of people for her son and for all the troops. But that was not possible, and so she tried to draw a mental picture. It was two o'clock in the morning in Germany, and she couldn't sleep. Her excitement could not be contained as she thought about God receiving these hundreds of prayers all at one time. She could only imagine in her wildest dreams how God would answer those prayers.

It was close to 8:00 p.m. The TV reporters had arrived; they wanted to talk to me for a few minutes, and a few minutes was all I had to give as the time was drawing near for the program to begin. One reporter guessed there were at least 500 people present. I was sure he was right. I couldn't believe it. The evening was everything and so much more than we could have hoped for.

We began with Toby Keith's song, "American Soldier." The words were so appropriate and the melody was so strong. "I'm an American soldier, an American. Beside my brothers and my sisters, I will proudly take a stand. When liberty's in jeopardy, I will always do what's right. I'm out here on the front lines, sleep in peace tonight. American soldier, I'm an American soldier." It made me choke up so badly, and then I decided I might as well forget about holding back the tears. As the color guard presented the colors and stood at attention with the reflection of the sun setting on the water in the background, we said the Pledge of Allegiance to the Flag and then sang the National Anthem. The air was filled with patriotism, emotion, and love.

I took the podium. Much to my surprise, I wasn't nervous. I looked out into the crowd of hundreds and saw so many people I didn't know. Some brought their own flags, and some had yellow ribbons and flag pins on their lapels. Most of the people were dressed in red, white, and blue, and all of them were ready to sing and pray with all their might for those defending our freedom. I was so moved. I glanced down at the program and looked at John's photo on the cover. He's such a handsome young man, and I love him so much. "God, please give me wisdom to say what you want me to say tonight." Before I began, I turned the program over to read the Guidepost Ministries "Prayer for America's Troops." It was so appropriate. "Dear Lord, hold our troops in Your loving hands. Protect them as they protect us. If they are tired, give them strength. If they are wounded and suffering, give them comfort. If they are lonely, touch them with Your gentle hand and let them know You are near them. Grant them strength and wisdom. Comfort and uplift the hearts of the families who await the return of their loved ones. Amen."

This program was given to those who attended the prayer vigil.

The following words were written below John's photo on the front of the program. "The world situation in these times affects all of us. Although we are not on the front lines in combat, we can all be on the front lines in prayer. Reaching out to God in prayer for comfort, strength, and safety for all our troops and their families is something everyone can do." This was what we did that night. We reached out our hands to God, and He filled them with all His wonders.

John's nephew, Jeffrey, prayed earnestly for his uncle.

I started my remarks by welcoming everyone and thanking those who had made a contribution to the evening's program. John Borsa, a reporter with Channel 7 News in Buffalo, had become our friend.

Earlier that day, during a phone call I made to Philip in Germany, John Borsa and his staff graciously taped a message from Philip to be played at the vigil. The time had come to hear Phil's message. Even though Phil's voice was choked with emotion, he managed to speak.

"It's just unbelievable. No words can explain how we feel. People can't forget that this isn't just about my brother. This is about all the soldiers who are over there, who are wounded and who are fighting for our freedom. He is a warrior and he's going to make it." There wasn't a dry eye in the crowd. We were all overcome with emotion.

Next was my update on John's condition and some of the thoughts and feelings John had previously shared with Philip in their telephone conversations just a few weeks before John was injured. I told everyone what Risë told me when I talked with her on my cell phone just a few minutes earlier. "A social worker at the hospital told me today that based on what he has seen and heard about prayers for John and what is happening with John's condition, he now knows that he has definitely seen the power of God." Even John's doctors and nurses in Germany were in awe!

Next I invited Senator Maziarz to the podium to say a few words about his experience with making it possible for Phil and Stephanie to get their passports in New York City and then making sure they arrived at LaGuardia in time for their flight to Germany the previous Sunday. As he walked to the podium, the crowd began to cheer and applaud, and everyone rose to their feet in a standing ovation. He shared his thoughts. "It was an experience. I think that God does work sometimes in strange ways. Ruth called me and said, 'I need passports and they're leaving on a plane tomorrow,' and I'm thinking, it takes at least ten days to two weeks to get a passport. She told me the circumstances. I said to her exactly the way she quoted me. 'Well, let me make some calls.' I say that every time someone calls me. But, those calls, there wasn't a person that I called — Judge Kloch, Congressman Reynolds, Paul Smaldone, the Clerk of the Erie County Family Court, Judge Barbara Howe; there wasn't a person that I called who hesitated for a scintilla of a second, that didn't want to do something to help out. We can overcome this one. Of course, our problem was always that there was another roadblock, and we'd have to make another call and go from there. But it was a great experience, and something I know I'll never forget. But the important thing is that John comes home and comes home healthy, and that's why we're all here today. And I just want to say, Ruth, this is one great community that we have in Western New York. There are people calling me. Governor Pataki called me today when he heard about this. He wanted to know what he could do to help out. Our women and men in the military, we have them in our thoughts and our prayers constantly. We will bring them home, and we're going to bring John home, and we're going to bring him home healthy, and we are going to have a great barbecue." The crowd once again began cheering for the senator. What a good man he is, and our family will be forever grateful to him for all he did for us.

NYS Senator George D. Maziarz
at the prayer vigil.

LTC Van Roosen then told his "small world" story. I could tell people were amazed, and I noticed their crinkled brows. They were straining to comprehend the enormity of what the Lieutenant Colonel had just told them. The paths of two local soldiers had crossed on the same ground in a faraway land, and the grace of God had brought LTC Van Roosen to the prayer vigil to talk about it.

Pastor Moldenhauer then began his beautiful, heartfelt, and passionate prayers for John and for all our troops. He quoted scripture, and told stories about John and his family. Linda Robinson led us in song. As the sun went down, people began lighting their candles. The mood and setting were perfect in every way. I had never seen a more beautiful sight in my life. My heart was literally filled with emotion; I could feel it.

On this night, many were gathered to pray for John and for all our troops.

I ended my remarks with these comments. "John is the hero of our family, and we'd like to thank him for giving himself to our country when he entered the army on July 10, 2001 as he joined in the effort to protect the wonderful USA and make the world a more peaceful place. He is a brave man, and no matter what happens, God is in control and has a perfect plan for John's life." Our closing hymn, *Let*

There Be Peace on Earth, never sounded more beautiful or meant more to our family.

***Pastor Moldenhauer singing
"Let There Be Peace on Earth."***

The evening ended a little after 10:00 p.m. The candlelight had spread for blocks, and even the people in the boats passing slowly by behind the podium took part in the service. The heaviness of heart that people had come to the prayer vigil with had been lifted. We all had renewed hope and plenty of strength to carry on.

There were hundreds of prayers for John being sent up to God. Our serenity came from years of knowing that "faith is not believing that God can; it is knowing that God will." With each prayer request our heavenly Father received for John, He returned His peace to the faithful. Through that peace, God's message could be felt. "I am hearing your prayers, as I always do. I am with John, and I will not leave him. You can consider it done."

A HOSPITAL ... A HOME

by John

☆ ☆ ☆

Wednesday, July 28, 2004 - 11:40 p.m.
Bayji, Iraq

I have just been shot. With all of the confusion, it is taking a few minutes for the truck to get here and pick me up. Some of the guys want to come with me, but their orders are to stay put and keep watching for the enemy. All the shooting has stopped. The truck has arrived, and some of my fellow soldiers are putting me on a stretcher and putting me in the truck. The doors are closing, and we are taking off. Right now I don't feel any pain. I wonder if this means I'm in shock. I'm really scared.

We are racing back to FOB Summerall, which is about a mile away, but it feels like it is taking forever to get there. SSG Banuelos, SFC Ireland, SGT Hernandez, and SSG Manning are with me. We are making jokes and trying to keep the situation light. Hernandez won't let me close my eyes, and he keeps shaking my shoulder, trying to keep me awake. I want to go to sleep.

We quickly arrive at the aid station at FOB Summerall. My clothes are being cut off, and my wounds are being assessed. The medics here are great, and they will know what to do to help me. At that moment, I am most concerned that my private areas are intact, and I receive much comfort when the medic tells me I am okay in that area.

The shock must be wearing off. I am starting to feel incredible pain. I am begging for morphine. They finally get the morphine running into me, and my friend, Smith, the medic, is reminding me that I owe him money. "Don't think you're getting out of it this easy," he jokes. "You still owe me $130." 1SG Grinston keeps talking to me while they are working on me. He keeps telling me I'm not going to die.

I just want to go to sleep, but 1SG Grinston continues talking to me. "Pirinelli, you're going to make it. Hang on. Stay awake. Think positive. You're going to the field hospital at FOB Speicher in a few moments!"

"Okay. Can Victor go with me?"

"Pirinelli, it's SGT Hernandez, and yes, he can go with you." By saying this, my First Sergeant is gently reminding me that I need to respect SGT Hernandez' rank. Hernandez is my superior. I think what 1SG Grinston is really trying to do is maintain a "business as usual" atmosphere so I will stay calm.

"Thank you, sir."

"Can we go, please? I need to get to the hospital. Please. I can't stand this pain. I don't want to die. Please, don't let me die!!!!"

It feels like the medics must be running 50 miles an hour toward the helicopter as they carry me on a stretcher. I hear the noise of the rotating propellers of the Black Hawk, and I feel the wind on my face. The medics know how seriously I am injured. Something is telling me to stay calm and keep the faith. That seems a lot easier to do than be scared, so that is what I am going to do as much as I can.

Victor keeps talking to me, whispering in my ear, begging me to stay awake. I'm sure he thinks if I go to sleep, I will never wake up. Just a half hour ago, we were on a routine patrol. We even had a few laughs along the route. Now, I have the feeling my life will never be the same. We haven't gotten over losing our three buddies on Good Friday, and that horror is becoming too real again. I remember the day they died, thinking it could have been me that was killed, and now it might be me that dies.

The pain is starting to subside. The morphine is doing its job.

It takes about ten minutes to get to Speicher. While we are flying, Victor is doing a countdown for me, minute by minute, so I can have an idea of how much longer it will be before we get there. This will keep me occupied.

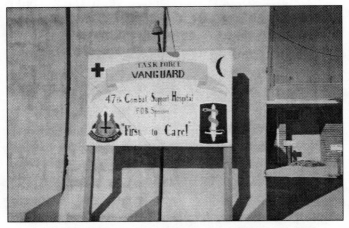

FOB Speicher, near Tikrit, was the first of the three hospitals I would call home for many weeks.

We have arrived at Speicher. I am being gurneyed into the operating room. The surgeon, Dr. Andrew Friedman, looks at me with all the calmness he can muster. He is ready to operate on me. I can see the compassion in his eyes, and I know I can trust him. "John, we will take care of you. You just concentrate on keeping a positive attitude. You are going into surgery in a few minutes so we can see what's going on inside of you."

I look at my left hand, and my wedding ring is gone. My clothes are gone that hold my guardian angel and my Soldier's Bible my parents gave me. I have had them with me since I arrived in Iraq, and now, when I need them the most, I don't have them. They are earthly things, and I think it's better if I talk directly to God.

My eyelids are getting so heavy, and, thank God, I don't feel any pain now. I am lying under some big lights. I hope Mom, Dad, and Katrin don't get too worried. Thanks, everybody, for everything you are doing for me. See you later.

Friday, August 6, 2004 – 3:30 a.m.

Landstuhl Regional Medical Center, Germany

Landstuhl Regional Medical Center was the second hospital I would call home after my injury.

"John, wake up. John, please wake up. There is a prayer vigil going on for you right now at home. Mom called Aunt Ruth and she told Mom that there are hundreds of people there. They are all praying for you to live. They are all asking God for a miracle for you. John, you're a warrior. You've been fighting for your life now for eight days, and you have to keep it up. Please, if you can hear me, open your eyes."

Eight days? Is that how long I've been here? That's Phil's voice I hear. With all my might, I try to open my eyes. Phil and Dad are so excited. Where am I, and what is going on? Is it day or night, and how did I get here? How long have I been sleeping? I'm so groggy. I want to talk to Phil, but I can't speak. I'm so glad he's here. He's telling me I'm a warrior. I've come so far. Jokingly he says to me, "Do you want me to kiss you?" As sick as I am, I feel like I want to tease my brother, as usual. I think I am nodding my head as if to say "no!"

"If you don't want me to kiss you, can Stephanie kiss you?" I must have shook my head yes, because the next thing I feel and see is Stephanie next to my face kissing me on the cheek. I can hear everyone crying and laughing at the same time.

Phil must think I may have changed my mind about him kissing me, because he is asking me again. The best reaction I can muster up for him, with Dad helping me to lift my arm and hand, is to give him the hand gesture I have in the past when we joke. I hear Phil saying, "Dad, did you see that? His brain is okay!"

Quickly, with all his excitement, Phil asks me, "John, what face did Grandpa Pirinelli make?"

I don't know if I can do it with this thing in my throat, but I will try to scrunch my upper lip to the right and my lower lip to the left. I wonder if he can see it, and if I really did it, or is this just in my mind?

I know I must have done it. Phil is jumping up and down next to my bed. Phil is telling me that Mom is at the Fisher House, and I should just hang on and try to stay awake. He's going to get her. I wonder where he thinks I am going. Phil better take it easy or he's going to end up in a hospital bed with a heart attack from all his excitement.

I can feel someone kissing my cheek, and I can hear Katrin's voice. I can't talk to her, and I can barely open my eyes, so I hope she doesn't leave me. It feels good to have her here. I remember begging the medics and the doctors to keep me alive so I could be with her and meet Little John when he is born. She tells me I am in the hospital in Germany.

I have a tube down my throat, and it is so uncomfortable. I don't feel any pain, but I can't move. I will try to open my eyes again just a little bit more so they know I am still with them. I think my eyelids just fluttered. I hope they saw it.

It seems like just seconds have gone by, but I know it has to be longer than that. Mom is in my room now, too. I am so glad she is here. I feel much safer now with her next to me, and her presence makes me feel stronger. Now I can break down a little. I'm so tired, and I'm so scared. What is that I feel on my face? I think it's my own tears. I must be crying. This must be pretty bad. God, please help me.

There are so many people standing around my bed. I hear Mom and Dad talking. I strain to see what's going on, but I can just barely lift one eyelid. I can see Dad standing next to my bed. He isn't saying anything, and I can see he is crying. Some of my doctors and nurses are standing around my bed holding hands, and Mom is praying for me and for them. I am thinking about a Bible verse I learned in confirmation class, Matthew 18:20. "For where two or three are gathered together in my name, there I am in the midst of them." I'll bet she's making them feel as good as she makes me feel when she prays for me. She is asking for God's wisdom and skill for them, and she is asking God to heal my body. She is telling them I have faith, and I do. I have had it as far back as I can remember. The doctors and nurses are so glad to hear that because, they say, they have better results with patients who have spiritual support and beliefs. I must be very badly hurt. I hear Stephanie's voice. She's a nurse, and she's helping to take care of me. I'm so tired.

I hear my doctors talking to Mom and Dad about my injuries. I have had three surgeries already, and I will have a fourth surgery today. I have lost one kidney, my liver is grazed, I have a piece of shrapnel next to my spine, and my intestines are severely injured. Many of my internal organs are exposed because my abdomen is a gaping hole. My body is swollen to almost twice its normal size. I have a blood infection. How in the world can I still be alive?

Sergeant Rodas, my social worker, is in my room. He is telling Mom and Dad that based on what he has seen so far with the improvement in my condition, he has now seen the power of God. God must really have something special in store for me. I wonder why I am still living when some of my really good buddies aren't. This isn't making any sense to me.

Saturday, August 7, 2004

Mom is coming into my room, and I mouth the words to her, "When can I go home." I see the sadness in her eyes and a smile on her face. She tells me I am making great progress, but I have to be patient. I don't think I'm going to die because I think if I was, Mom would probably be crying.

I feel a tiny bit more alert today, and I'm not sleeping quite as much now. I am still flat on my back, and I don't think I even want to know how many tubes are running in and out of my body. I think I heard my doctors saying I have a urinary tract catheter and a bag to collect my bodily waste. I think they called it an ileostomy. This must be the case because I don't get out of bed to go to the bathroom. I couldn't, even if I wanted to. There is so much machinery around me. Even when I can't see it, I can hear it working, and I think the machinery and God are keeping me alive.

I still have the tube in my throat, and I know now it is a respirator. Every time I wake up, the tube is filled with fluid. I feel like I'm drowning. The doctors and nurses keep suctioning the tube out, but I am so scared because sometimes I feel like I can't breathe. Someone from my family is always with me, and Dad has promised me that he will not leave my side until I come home. I hope I do go home someday.

I can mouth words, so at least I can communicate.

I hear the doctor telling Mom I will probably go to Walter Reed Army Medical Center in Washington,

D.C. on Monday on a medical transport plane. It will be interesting to see how this is going to work. My doctors are saying the swelling in my body is starting to go down significantly because my remaining kidney is starting to function more efficiently, and my lung sounds are better. I am still in critical condition. From what I can tell, I'm lucky to be alive. The doctors told Katrin when I got here a week ago that I had a 20% chance of survival. So far, so good. Thank you, Lord.

Mom told me how LTC McClelland and 1SG Grinston are calling the hospital every day from Iraq to see how I am because they are so worried about me. They are passing the daily updates on to my buddies who are anxiously awaiting news on my condition. They are worried about me, and I'm worried about them.

Sunday, August 8, 2004

I am definitely going to Walter Reed AMC tomorrow, and it will be so good to be on American soil again. Maybe then some of my family can visit me when I get a little better. I'm sure it won't be long before my Grandma Klein comes to see me in my new home at Walter Reed.

Dad and Phil will fly on the medi-vac plane with me. I don't think it's a good idea for Dad to fly with me, but no one can talk him out of it. Dad has a very bad back, and he's a diabetic. He tells me again that he isn't going to leave my side until I go home. I don't think I've ever seen such a soft side to my dad, and I can tell he feels so sorry for me. Dad and I haven't always seen eye to eye, but his unconditional love for me is very clear to me now.

Monday, August 9, 2004

I wonder how they are going to load me onto a bus and eventually onto a plane. I have so much equipment attached to me, and I am still lying flat on my back. My family is standing around my bed, and one of my nurses is going to take our picture. Mom, Dad, Phil, and Katrin are all smiling, and Katrin and I are cheek to cheek as she holds my face. They all look so tired, but their smiles are telling me I'm going to get better. I hope they aren't just real good actors. I'm so tired.

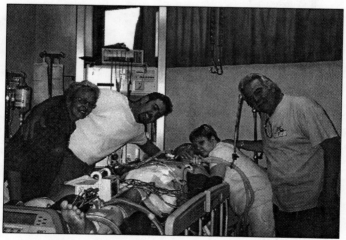

I could tell by the smiles of my family members that I was going to be okay.

Right before the medics put me on the bus that will take me and other wounded soldiers to the airport, I look over and see my mother crying. It is really hard for her to say "goodbye for now" to me even though it will only be a few days before I see her again in the U.S. Katrin is crying because I just mouthed to her the words, "Leave me alone!" I feel so overwhelmed when I look at her. She is pregnant and exhausted, and she won't leave my side. She is so devoted to me, and I feel guilty because I have done this to her. My emotions are playing tricks on me. I have to tell Katrin I'm sorry.

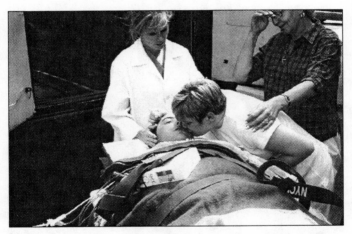

Katrin is kissing me goodbye before I got on the bus to go to the airport en route to Walter Reed. Nurse Michelle Hardin did a wonderful job of making this trip as easy as she could for me.

Mom will stay in Germany with Katrin and help her pack up our belongings in our apartment and get ready to move to the States, something we weren't planning to do until my scheduled return from Iraq around April 2005. But of course all those plans have now been drastically changed.

Phil puts his sunglasses on my face, and Mom takes a picture. All the medical personnel around us are laughing and crying at the same time. Dad and Phil get on the bus right after me, and, out of the corner of my eye, I can see them waving goodbye to Mom and Katrin. In my mind, I am telling Mom and Katrin I love them, and I will see them soon. I am worried about Katrin because she hasn't eaten or slept in days. She has to stay healthy for herself and our baby, and I can see that we have a long road ahead of us.

We have arrived at the airport, and I am being loaded onto the plane. There are four beds with seriously wounded soldiers in them. I am in one of those beds. The soldiers who are in better shape are in beds stacked up three high.

I feel the urge to cough again because of the fluids collecting in the trach tube. The nurse will get Phil, and I will hold onto his arm for strength. Coughing hurts me so badly, and coughing scares me because there is so much fluid caught in the trach tube, and I never know if I am going to be able to breathe when I am done coughing. I'm so glad Phil is here to help me.

It won't be long before I am sedated. I won't wake up again until we are in Washington. I look at the orange, basket-like seats hanging on the walls inside the plane. I can't believe Dad and Phil are going to sit in those seats for hours and hours, just so they can be with me. They must really love me. I know I really love them.

Stephanie will take another flight back to the States, and I will see her again when we get to Washington.

Tuesday, August 10, 2004

Walter Reed Army Medical Center

We have arrived at Walter Reed Army Medical Center in Washington, DC, and now this is my new home. I don't remember anything from the flight, but I guess it must have been a little too much for me. I have to go back into surgery again, and I've lost count of how many surgeries this makes. In addition to losing one of my kidneys, my intestines have been severely damaged. This part of my injury is very serious because much of the injury is in my duodenum (the beginning part of my intestines), and I can't live without it. I now have something on the hole in my abdomen I have never heard of. It is called a wound vac. It is a medicated sponge placed into the hole. It has a cover on it with a tube coming out of it that will drain all the impurities and promote healing. I can't imagine how long it is going to take this huge hole to close.

A team of seven doctors has visited me a couple of times today already. They have told me they will continue this routine until I leave the hospital. When I hear them talk, I am amazed at their knowledge. I am thinking such scary things about my physical condition as I ask my questions by mouthing words to them, and they are calming me as they patiently give me their explanations and answers.

Dad and Phil will stay at the Fisher House. It's about three miles from the hospital. They will check in at the Fisher House while I am in surgery because they want to get back to the hospital before I come back to ICU from Recovery. Stephanie is staying with her aunt who lives near the hospital, but she assures me she will come to the hospital to see me every day.

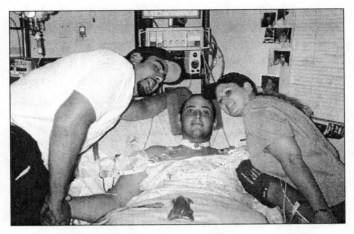

Phil and Stephanie were always by my side.

Here come the orderlies. I am getting used to the surgery routine now. Now that I think about it, I think this is surgery number six.

I'm so tired.

Wednesday, August 11, 2004

Today I am being taken off the respirator. What if I can't breathe when it is off? I'm scared, and I will have to trust my doctors and God that nothing will happen to me today that God and I can't take care of together.

All goes well, and now I'm breathing on my own. Stephanie continues to reassure me that I am doing well. She is a good nurse. I have seen that for myself, and I trust everything she tells me.

A psychiatrist has come to see me today. He asks me a lot of questions, and I communicate with him the best way I can, by mouthing words. He says I am doing very well in light of all I have gone through in the last two weeks. He assures me it is normal for me to feel so physically, emotionally, and mentally exhausted, and I should continue to concentrate on getting better. A good mental attitude and family support will work wonders for me, and he assures me he will be stopping by regularly to see me. I really don't want to talk to him. I feel like he can't possibly know what I am going through.

I hear one of my doctors saying that the skill of Dr. Friedman at FOB Speicher probably saved my life. There was a specialized procedure that had to be performed on my duodenum immediately after my injury. God performed a miracle when he entered Dr. Friedman's mind and gave him the skill and wisdom to do just the right thing in that operating room. I am so grateful!

I also hear the doctors saying it has only been 13 days since I was injured, and they cannot believe the rapid progress I am making in my recovery. Less than two weeks ago, I had a 20% chance of survival. Today I am breathing on my own, and an assessment of my mental state seems pretty positive to me. Thank you, God!

Friday, August 13, 2004

Grandma Klein, Aunt Ruth, and Cousin Kristy are coming to see me today. I will give them a big smile when they get here. They have been so worried about me.

I can sit up a little more now. I still have the same amount of tubes running in and out of me, and I am learning the names of all of them since I am awake a lot more these days.

I have my own room in ICU and my own nurse 24 hours a day. I guess you have to be pretty sick to get all that attention. All my doctors are great, but Dr. Peoples is my primary doctor, and I have a lot of trust and faith in him. He says that my visitors will be good for me, and my family is good medicine. Before he leaves my room, he reduces my tracheotomy and puts a flap on it so I can talk now, just in time to say hi to my grandmother. She will be surprised, and so will everyone else.

Here come Grandma, Aunt Ruth, and Kristy. Oh, I don't know how I feel about this. I am starting to feel anxious. How can this be? These are people in my life I love. I say, "Grandma, sit down over here," and I hear gasps from everyone in the room. This is the first time I have talked since my injury, and everyone is ecstatic. Why don't I feel ecstatic? I just feel anxious.

We talk for a while, and then they leave with the promise of coming back later. I can hear them talking to Dr. Peoples in the hallway, and he is explaining my injuries and progress in healing to them. I can only hear a few words here and there, but it all sounds good to me.

When they come back, Aunt Ruth asks me if I want to watch the video from the prayer vigil. She thinks it may lift my spirits, seeing all those hundreds of people praying for a miracle for me. What is wrong with me? I don't want to watch it, but I don't want to hurt her feelings, so we watch it for a few minutes. My nurse comes in and watches with us for a few minutes, and then he remarks I am one lucky guy to have all those people praying for me. "No wonder you are getting well so fast," he says. We turn it off. Maybe we'll watch more later on.

I think everyone can sense this is too much for me. I feel like everything is closing in on me. Is this claustrophobia? My logical mind tells me it can't be, but I think I may have some of the symptoms. I don't want to hurt anyone's feelings, so I hope they will leave soon. They do, and I can see they are okay with that. They just want what is going to make me happy.

Grandma can hardly look at me without bursting into tears. Aunt Ruth is keeping her distance. She doesn't want to upset me. I think she can tell I am tense, and she doesn't want to put any stress on me.

It is time to change the wound vac over the opening in my abdomen. I hope the opening is getting smaller. It has already shrunk to a size a little bigger than the bottom of a three-pound coffee can. Kristy is going to stay in the room with me while Dr. Kim changes it. It is pretty painful, and I'm glad Kristy is here with me. Dr. Kim asks Kristy if she works in the medical field, because looking at what is under a wound vac is very hard to do if you're not used to it. Kristy tells Dr. Kim that she is used to medical procedures. I ask Dr. Kim if I am going to be able to have more children. She assures me that won't be a problem unless I intend to carry them in my abdomen. We all laugh, and I feel much better. I want Little John to have a brother or sister to grow up with.

At Walter Reed, the staff is extremely supportive of family being with the sick and injured, and I sure am glad. Kristy will stay with me tonight, and she is promising me we will have fun. This will be a first for me since July 28. Since we were very young, Kristy and I have kept everything "rocking and rolling" in the family, and I can see she's ready to lift my spirits. Kristy has a way of making every situation in life okay, no matter what it is. She cracks her jokes and actually makes me laugh. She takes some pictures of us making faces at the camera, and it feels really good to have her here. When we quiet down, I think for a few moments that every member of my family is helping me in a different way. It's amazing how it all works together. Eventually we both manage to sleep for a while.

Saturday, August 14, 2004

Mom and Katrin are still in Germany packing our belongings and getting Katrin's visa. I don't know when they will get here, and I sure do miss them.

Grandma, Aunt Ruth, and Kristy are still here, and I hear them out in the hallway talking with Dr. Peoples again. He is telling them what he told me yesterday. His biggest concern with my health is with my duodenum, the beginning section of my small intestine. It has to heal, and it cannot be removed. The reason I have an ileostomy is so my intestines can rest and heal. I am very lucky, because it sounds like I won't have this bag collecting my body waste for the rest of my life. If all goes well, I could leave the hospital in about two months with nothing more than a scarred belly and one less kidney.

Dr. Peoples has made my day. He tells my family that out of the 3,000+ soldiers he has treated, my healing and recovery is one of the fastest he has seen. If I keep progressing like I have so far, my only limitation should be I wouldn't be able to play contact sports like football anymore. That's okay, because I plan to take up golf and play regularly with all the golfers in my family.

It has only been a little over two weeks since I was injured and on death's doorstep, and God is really blessing me. Why do I feel so tense? I think I will go to sleep for a while.

Sunday, August 15, 2004

Today, Grandma, Aunt Ruth, and Kristy are going home, and Stephanie will go with them. She must be really anxious to get home. She has been right by my side since this whole ordeal began, and her nursing skills have been a benefit to me. She is more like a sister to me than a sister-in-law.

My visitors stay in my room for about 10 minutes and then they leave for 45 minutes. I don't feel as anxious now. Phil is going to stay with me a couple more weeks, but I am worried his employer is going to start to lose patience with him. He assures me all is well with his job. He just can't seem to pull himself away from me for very long. This is brotherly love at its best! Boy, am I lucky.

Mom and Katrin are still in Germany working out some details. I sure do wish they would get here soon. My dad, brother, and Stephanie are great, but I am finding out my mom is where my superhuman strength comes from. I guess it is really coming from God through her, and she has such a great way of making sure it "fills me up."

Before Aunt Ruth leaves, she asks me if she can take my picture while I'm on the phone talking to Katrin. This is a milestone as I've only been able to talk since the day before yesterday. I give Aunt Ruth a smile, and that makes her very happy! I can just imagine what she's going to do with that digital photo when she gets home. I'll bet it will be sent out with Janet's next email to hundreds of people. I get a little embarrassed, but I'll get over it.

They are all so happy I'm getting better, and they want to spread the good news. When you see a miracle unfolding before your eyes, this is news that should be shared, but I am still having a hard time comprehending the miracle part. I wish I didn't feel so down because I have so much to be thankful for.

Some food sure would taste good. I wonder when this feeding tube will be taken out.

I'm so tired.

Wednesday, August 18, 2004

Today I will receive the Purple Heart from the Army. I have been told Walter Reed Memorial Health

Care Systems Commander Jim Gilman is presenting the award to me. My Aunt Ruth is at home making plans for photographs to be taken and emailed to her right after the presentation. One of my nurses, Susan Murray, has offered to take digital photos and email them to Aunt Ruth, and I still can't believe everything people are doing for me. Kristy's husband, Wally, is here, too. He was kind enough to drive a car here so my family will have transportation while they are in Washington. He will fly home to New York in a couple days.

Commander Gilman is very sincere in his remarks. He is a gentleman, he is dedicated to his job, and I respect him. Lots of photos are taken, and my brother tells me they will be on the Buffalo, New York TV stations tonight. I can't wait until this is over. I feel bad when I think like that. What is wrong with me? I just want to go to sleep.

The Buffalo TV news crew is down at the main gate of the hospital waiting to talk to Dad and Phil because they are not allowed to enter the hospital grounds. It's hard for me to take all this attention. I still believe the real heroes are all the soldiers who have lost their lives. I'm still alive, and I'm going to be okay, so I think all the credit and awards should be going to them.

My father is so emotional. He told me what he said to the reporters. "I have never shed so many tears in my life for anything or anyone. And today the tears were from happiness — all joy. Every tear that came out of my eyes was joy because my son is okay."

Philip told me what he said. "I'm just so proud of my brother and proud of these soldiers and what they're doing over there. Every soldier that I've talked to here wants to go back to Iraq, can't wait to go back because of the good we're doing."

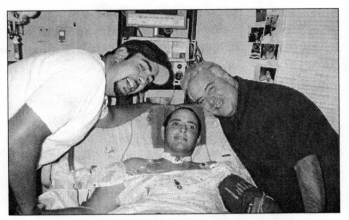

Phil, Dad, and me with the Purple Heart on my chest.

I'm so glad the Purple Heart presentation is over. I will sleep now.

Thursday, August 19, 2004

Today is a great day for me. Mom and Katrin have finally arrived in Washington. I missed them terribly, and it is so good to see them. I am feeling better already. I would never want Dad and Phil to think I don't appreciate everything they are doing for me, but Mom, well…she's my mom. Once I can see

Katrin and see that she's okay, I know that will make me feel better, too. I am worried about her and our baby she is carrying.

Katrin is staying at the Mologne House right next to the hospital. Mom is going to the Fisher House with Dad and Phil. I have heard the Fisher House is very comforting to my family. So many of their needs are met there, and that makes me feel much better. I am still having a hard time comprehending everything being done for me. I'm so tired.

Friday, August 20, 2004

Today is another super day, and I am elated I am having two good days in a row. I am spending today getting caught up with Mom and Katrin, and so I think I will just lay here and look at them. They are a sight for sore eyes. I ask them to please not stand over my bed. For some reason it really bothers me, and I'm not sure why.

My mother continues her ritual of putting holy water on me. It makes her feel better because she thinks of it as a point of contact with God, and I have to admit, it makes me feel better, too. No wonder I missed her so much. I think I will take a nap now.

When I wake up, I hear more good news. I am being moved to a regular room today, my new home. I must be doing really well as the doctor has also removed one of my drain tubes, and my tracheotomy has been downsized. It won't be long before it is gone forever. I will sleep now.

I awake to the news that I need a CT scan. My blood pressure is low, and I have some fluid in my lungs. My bed is larger than most because I am so big, and the nurses are having a hard time getting me out of my room. One of my tubes is being pulled. I am so angry because it hurts so badly. I will have to tell them I am sorry for snapping at them.

After a bit of a wait, I find out the results are good, and this setback is something minor. I feel very nervous every time something with my medical condition changes. Sometimes I feel like I'm walking on a tightrope. I wish I could just relax.

I will think good thoughts. It has now been three and a half weeks since I was given a 20% chance to live, and that's not very long to go from death's doorstep to a regular hospital room. It is a miracle, and I thank you, God.

I'm so tired.

Sunday, August 22, 2004

Dad stayed with me again last night. I have watched him sit in a chair and sleep now for weeks, night after night, even though I know his back must really be hurting. He straightened my room up this morning as usual and went to church at the hospital chapel with Katrin, Mom, and Phil. This has been their ritual since I have been at Walter Reed. They report to me each week how the pastor and those in attendance pray for the soldiers in the hospital as well as for all America's troops. It gives me a good feeling to know that my family continues to worship, even though they are not at home.

Monday, August 23, 2004

Today I will have sonograms on my legs to make sure I don't have any blood clots. I have to get out of bed, and I hope my tubes don't get pulled again. I'm going to stand for a few moments and then sit in the chair in my room. This will help my lungs clear of fluid and get my circulation going a little bit better. I can't keep lying in this bed. It has been three and a half weeks since I was injured, and I need to get moving.

It is amazing what I have learned about medicine. I know the name and function of every tube going in and out of me. I am continually watching how things are done for me. I may as well learn something while I'm lying here. My team of doctors continues their daily routine of coming to see me twice every day.

I have been feeling more like myself the last few days. I'm not sure what to attribute that to. It could be medication, or I'm just getting better. I won't ponder it for too long. I am just grateful.

Phil just told me that he is going home on Wednesday. I feel a bit of a jolt from that news. He's been with me constantly for four weeks. I will miss him, but he has to get home to his wife and his job. I think I am "over the hump." Thank you, God.

Tuesday, August 24, 2004

Cousin Janet has forwarded an email to my mother that she received from 1SG Grinston. "Dear Janet, this is First Sergeant Grinston here in Iraq, and I wanted to say thank you for the updates on John. John has many friends here in his unit, and we are all concerned about his health. I print your updates and pass them out to the soldiers. Your updates boost my soldiers' morale, knowing that John is doing better. Thank you for the information. Please tell John we are fine, and we are still thinking about him."

I'm having a hard time with all this attention. My army buddies are still there in harm's way, and they are worried about me. They are my family, too. Dear, God, please protect all the soldiers in Iraq. For some, it will be Your will for them to come to heaven with You. For me, it was not, and I thank You as I will be here for the birth of my son. Thank you, God.

I'm so tired.

Thursday, August 26, 2004

Army Chaplain John Kallerson visited me again today. I find myself telling him things I would never tell anyone else. Maybe part of the reason is because he has experienced combat, just like I have, and because he is such a Christian man. I feel a connection with him that is very comforting. I look forward to his visits.

Today Chaplain Kallerson brought me a quilt his wife made for me. I have never met her, but I'm sure she must be as good a person as he is.

Friday, August 27, 2004

Pretty soon the doctors are going to change my wound vac again. This is the one procedure that I dislike the most. Every time it is changed, I receive anesthesia. I hope all the doses of anesthesia aren't damaging my body even more. So far, the only good part of this procedure is how the doctors are always amazed when they take the wound vac off my abdomen and see the miraculous healing taking place underneath it. The opening in my abdomen is getting smaller and smaller. I hope it won't be long before they can close me up. My doctors tell me they can't believe how fast I am healing, and this report makes me feel really good.

Something big is about to happen right after this. My doctor is going to take my catheter out. I am scared. What if I can't urinate? They will have to put it back in. The more I dwell on it, the harder it is going to be to urinate. My nurses have been telling me I have to retrain my bladder, and I'm trying.

The catheter is out. The wound vac has been changed. It wasn't quite as painful this time. Now I will wait and hope that soon I will feel the sensation to urinate. I have to stay calm. Maybe I'll go to sleep for a while. Before I drift off to sleep, I wonder if my body's other waste elimination function will return to normal someday when this bag can be removed. I must be patient.

It's late. I can tell because it is dark outside. I am waking up, and my first thought is I don't have a catheter anymore. I feel like I have to urinate, and my nurse helps me. Praise the Lord, all systems are working. I feel like I'm a little boy again, but I have to call Mom and Katrin and tell them. This is another giant step toward getting out of this bed and going home. Thank you, God! As low as I feel at times, I can't help but smile.

Sunday, August 29, 2004

My mother is flying home tonight. She hasn't been home for a month. I know she doesn't want to leave me, but she needs to get home for a while and go back to work for a few days. I will be all right, but I will miss her. I try not to make her feel guilty. I know she wouldn't leave me if she thought there were going to be any dramatic changes for the worse in my condition.

Once again, Mom leaves the holy water duties for Dad. "Don't miss a day," she tells him, "and, John, make sure you say your prayers when Dad is putting the water on you." We both nod our heads up and down because we fully understand how important this ritual is to her. It's very important to us, too. As Mom explains, she thinks of the holy water as a point of contact with God, just like my guardian angel and Soldier's Bible were for me when I was in Iraq. It is all good.

It would be so nice to eat something, and I am looking forward to that day. I hope I keep progressing so that when Mom comes back next weekend, she will be pleasantly surprised.

Wednesday, September 1, 2004

I am feeling sorry for being so gruff with my nurses today. I will have to apologize. I think it is hard for them to understand what I am going through, but they do their best to take care of all my needs, and they are good nurses.

I am never short with 1LT Haley and 1LT Simmons, two of my male nurses that I can relate to the best. 1LT Haley keeps Dad and me supplied with good movies, and 1LT Simmons loves Dad's and my jokes. The care they provide is also very good.

Friday, September 3, 2004

I am going to walk today. It is time, but I feel very dizzy. My nurse tells me dizziness is to be expected because I have been lying in bed for five weeks. I have lost 60 pounds, and I can tell I have lost a lot of muscle already. When I was in Iraq, there wasn't much to do other than work out when we weren't on a mission, sleeping, or eating. All that working out may have saved my life.

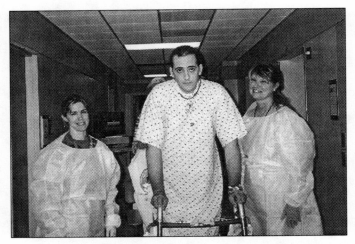

I am taking my first walk since my injury.

Mom, Aunt Ruth, Grandma, Philip, and Stephanie are coming to visit me tonight, and I can't wait to see them. They will perk me up. Dad and Katrin take really good care of me, and I am never alone.

I am tired. I think I will sleep.

I'm awake now, and I don't feel good. Dad is going to get my nurse. Something is very wrong with me; I am having a hard time breathing. The doctors and nurses are rushing in, and they are preparing me for some tests. I am paralyzed with fear.

My tests are done, and my doctor is coming to tell me the results. The bottom lobe of one of my lungs has collapsed, and I have blood clots in both my lungs. I was doing so well. Why is this happening to me? I am so scared, and I feel like I am going to throw up. I do. I feel very warm, and I think I have a fever. Yes, it's about 101. What is wrong with me?

It's 11:30 p.m. Here comes Mom, and I'm so glad she is here. She kisses me, gets a quick assessment of what is going on, and goes back to the car to tell Grandma and Aunt Ruth to come in. They aren't going to the Fisher House right now because I need Mom with me.

I feel my emotions slipping, and I am on that tightrope again. I think I am going to fall off this time. I'm so glad Mom will talk to the doctors. She does just that and then tells me what is happening is not really as bad as it sounds. Mom and Dad will stay with me tonight. Mom gets the holy water and dabs some on me, just for good measure. Katrin needs to get some sleep. She doesn't want to leave me, but I finally convince her to go. Aunt Ruth and Grandma also leave, and Mom, Dad, and I pray. Philip and Stephanie don't know anything about my current condition because they are staying with Stephanie's aunt who lives near Washington. I'm glad they can get a good night's sleep because who knows what tomorrow will bring.

I can't stand being so afraid. This fear makes me very angry. I'm not being moved back to ICU, so my medical condition must not be too serious. With that thought, I drift off to sleep for a while.

Saturday, September 4, 2004

I feel a bit better now. My fever is coming down, but I'm still throwing up. I think I'll try to get into a wheelchair today and go outside for some fresh air and see if that helps. My doctor doesn't seem too concerned, so that is a good sign. I'm so tired.

Janet has sent an email prayer request out for me. She has forwarded this email response from LTC McClelland, my commander in Iraq, to me. "Janet, I had a sense something was awry. I have some enter-tainer friends as I think I mentioned. Country singer Chely Wright visited Walter Reed yesterday. She was going to personally see John and deliver a message for me. Well, she tried four times, but each time the doctors said that John could not have visitors. Thank you for the update. A chaplain at the hospital has an autographed picture of Chely for John when he is better. The First Lightning Team will continue to keep Big John in our daily thoughts and prayers. Keep the faith."

I'm sorry I wasn't able to meet LTC McClelland's friend. I know he wanted me to, and it was so thoughtful of him to try to arrange it. I will have to tell him I am appreciative when I feel better. I just don't feel good. I feel so sad sometimes, and I don't know why. I hope it goes away soon.

Mom and Dad are really tired today. I better pray for them and forget about myself for a while. Katrin is doing pretty well, and I'm thankful for that. She has to stay healthy for the baby as the due date for the baby's birth is still a couple months away.

Sunday, September 5, 2004

Mom was supposed to go home today with Aunt Ruth, Grandma, Phil and Stephanie, but she is going to stay with me until the doctors figure out what is going on with me. I'm so glad. My doctors have ordered a CT scan of my abdomen, and my parents are helping put me on the table. After a short wait, I find out that everything looks good, but I still need more tests. My doctor has me on an antibiotic. He thinks I may have an infection somewhere. I feel so sad, and I just want to go to sleep. I want my family with me, but I don't. That seems pretty crazy to me. What is going on? I am so tired.

Monday, September 6, 2004

I feel a little better today. My doctors still haven't figured out what is going on, but several very serious suspected complications have been ruled out. The doctors are very concerned about the healing of my duodenum because I need it to live.

I am sitting in my chair today because I can't just lay here in this bed and wait for something to happen. It is making me feel very tense and anxious. Getting into the chair is a real project. There are so many tubes running in and out of me and so much equipment to be moved. It makes me very nervous because I am always worried about something being unplugged. I will have to continue to depend on God and the skill of my doctors and nurses. So far they haven't let me down.

Mom is telling me a story about how when Dad, Mom, Katrin and I were driving throughout Europe, with Dad and me in the front seat, and Mom and Katrin in the back seat, she would look at the back of my head and see the crease that always appeared to be a smile. She is noticing now, because of my weight loss, the crease is gone. She is anxious for me to be healthy again and gain some weight back, and then she will see the smile on the back of my head! And of course the addition of a smile on my face will make her life complete!

Another big problem has arisen today. Katrin had to see her doctor at the National Naval Medical Center in Bethesda, Maryland, because she is having contractions. The doctor has put her on some medication, and she can't do much walking. Our little boy is pretty big and she is small, so she really needs to take it easy. She is also dehydrated because she rarely leaves my side, and she is suffering from a lot of stress because of me. She needs to carry the baby at least four more weeks. She has got to start taking better care of herself and stop worrying so much about me. I will have to try to pull it together a little more, for her sake.

Tuesday, September 7, 2004

My brother, Rob, has come from his home in Cleveland, Ohio, to visit with me. He and my sister-in-law, Tracey, and my niece, Gabby, came to see me the first weekend I was at Walter Reed, and now he has made the trip again. It is good to see him, but I am still having a hard time with visitors. I don't want my brother to feel bad, but I can't help it.

Physically, I feel much better today. My doctors figured out what was making me throw up. They made a few changes in my medications, and I am relieved it has stopped.

Wednesday, September 8, 2004

Mom and Rob had to take Katrin to Bethesda in the middle of the night because Katrin started having contractions again. Dad stayed with me. I feel so sorry for my parents because of everything we are putting them through. They are still smiling and willing to do whatever has to be done, but I am worried that the straw that will finally break the camel's back, so to speak, is just around the corner. "God, my parents need you now more than ever." I don't know why I'm telling God what I'm sure He already knows. It's just so easy to talk to Him.

Katrin is now wheelchair bound. She has to continue the medication the doctor put her on to stop the contractions and she really has to take it easy. For many reasons, we aren't ready for Little John to come into the world yet.

Even though Mom is exhausted, she is showing me a lot of the newspaper articles from back home and sharing stories with me about all the wonderful acts of kindness my family is receiving. It's hard for me to imagine so many people are so worried about Katrin, my parents, and me. So, for all those supporters, I'm going to get out of this bed and walk at least 50 feet today. No, I need to do that 50 and another 50 for all those people who are praying for me. It feels good to get out of my room and see what is going on outside that door. It's more medicine, doctors, nurses, wounded and sick soldiers, and equipment, but it is different.

I don't feel so anxious today. Things are looking up. I need to think about Katrin, the baby, and my parents more than myself.

Thursday, September 9, 2004

I am feeling even better today. I think a 300-foot walk is in order.

Because of Katrin's condition, Mom is not going back home for a while. We are thankful she will be here with us because we really need her. I don't know how she and Dad are taking all this stress, but they continue to have smiles on their faces.

We are still not ready for Little John to come into the world, and I hope he stays put for a while.

Saturday, September 11, 2004

I have a fever today. I wonder what's going on now. My doctor just told me I have fluid on one of my lungs and it has to be drained. They are also going to insert a CVP line so they don't have to keep poking me while they figure out what is going on.

I am worried about my kidney function. Sometimes antibiotics can slow the function down. I will ask God to keep it going.

I am getting weary.

Thursday, September 16, 2004

Mom is going home tonight for a few days, but thankfully she'll be coming back on Monday. I feel like we need her now more than ever with Katrin's condition, but I have to let her go.

Friday, September 17, 2004

I will take another walk today, and I feel I'm getting stronger. Katrin is also holding her own. We're not ready for Little John to be born yet.

I started physical therapy last week, and I enjoy it. I wheel myself to the elevator, go to PT, and when I get back, I walk around the floor my room is on. Tuesday I went outside for a while, and it was good to get out of the hospital, breathe some fresh air, and feel the sunshine. This is a first for me since this whole ordeal began.

I always looked forward to my physical therapy.

Before I was a patient here, I heard a lot about Walter Reed Army Medical Center. I have never seen it, but I find out the picture I have in my mind is pretty accurate. The buildings are tan brick and concrete, and they are immense. Soldiers are everywhere, and every evening Taps is played when the flag is lowered. There is a serene courtyard and very well-kept grounds for people to enjoy. I am impressed.

I see a great number of soldiers who have lost their limbs in wheelchairs. The sight of these brave men and women makes me realize how fortunate I am. I know my injuries are very serious, and as I get older, I'm not sure how this will affect me, but for now, I consider myself a very lucky man.

Every week the doctors meet with my family to discuss my progress and treatments. At this week's family meeting, I found out I will probably be here for another month. The doctors are hoping to close the wound in my abdomen in the next couple weeks, and I will need skin grafts when the time comes.

I don't feel as depressed as I did a few weeks ago. I think my emotions are healing as quickly as my body is. I am excited about the upcoming birth of my son, and I even feel like telling a joke or two.

Brigadier General Bergner and Acting Secretary of the Army Les Brownlee came to see me this week. Country Singer Hank Brake also came to see me. I felt very honored by these visits.

I have nicknamed Dr. Jeff Seebach "The Butcher." He just laughs when I call him that. Sometimes I shorten his nickname and just call him "Butch." He takes really good care of me, and more importantly, I trust him. We are developing a very close relationship.

"Butch," my doctor, my friend.

Monday, September 20, 2004

Mom is coming back to Washington today. I am having surgery tomorrow to close the wound in my abdomen. This is surgery number eight, and I can't wait to get rid of this wound vac and one more tube. I still have many tubes left, and I won't count them.

Tuesday, September 21, 2004

Good news today. My surgery went great, and the wound on my abdomen has been closed. I didn't need skin grafts because the doctors were able to stretch my skin over the rest of the opening. I am closed up now. I am feeling a lot of pain, and I'm very sleepy. I hope my doctors decide to keep me sedated until this pain subsides.

It seems I will stay on the road to recovery. I have recently learned a soldier from my sister unit in Iraq was killed this week. Another soldier has died, and I am still living and getting better every day. It has been eight weeks since I was injured. God has a plan for my life, and I wonder what it is.

Saturday, September 25, 2004

My cousin, Risë, her husband, Rich, and their son, Evan, have made the trip down here to see me. I am glad to see them, but I am having trouble breathing. Once again, I can't even show them my appreciation. It seems like every time someone from home comes to see me, I get sick. I don't understand. These visits should make me feel better. They have decided to go home tomorrow so I can rest. Someday I will make it up to them.

A few weeks ago when some relatives from Pennsylvania came to visit me, the same thing happened. One of them, John Brink, served his country on the beaches of Normandy, and he understands better than most what I am going through.

Their visit was cut short because I started with a new medical problem.

I think I will sleep now and let my body and mind rest.

Monday, September 27, 2004

I am still suffering with complications. I am losing a lot of blood from around the two drain tubes in the incision in my abdomen, and I may need a blood transfusion. I thought I had come further than this.

I am so scared.

My doctors have clamped off another drain tube in preparation for its removal, but now I am throwing up. They will unclamp the tube for now and try it again in a few days. I hope I don't get sick when they clamp it again.

Katrin is still hanging in there, and, thankfully, my parents haven't had to rush her to the hospital recently. I thank God for that.

Wednesday, September 29, 2004

I had to have a blood transfusion today, and the drains in my incisions were also replaced.

I guess I spoke too soon. Katrin had to go back to the hospital last night as the contractions began again. She is taking a new medication, and hopefully it will stop the contractions.

Saturday, October 2, 2004

Cousin Janet received the following email from 1LT Willette Balsamo, one of my nurses at the hospital in Germany. She forwarded it to my mom so I could read it. "Hi, Janet. Thanks so much for the continued updates on John. I think of him and the family often, and it's terrific to get news on his continued successes. He's such a miracle. I'm so excited about the baby coming. The baby will be a wonderful help in his healing because he'll have the new little one to focus on and give him renewed strength to continue to recover. My prayers to all." This nurse's dedication to me is amazing. I'm sure many other soldiers have gone through Landstuhl since I was there, so it's hard for me to believe she even remembers who I am.

I am honored.

Monday, October 4, 2004

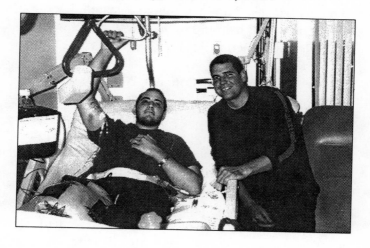

My visit with LT Leonard helped me reconnect with my buddies in Iraq. He went back to Iraq shortly after our visit.

Thursday, October 7, 2004

I just keep getting better and better. It has been ten weeks since I was injured. Today the doctors will remove the drain tube in my abdomen at the site of my major injury to my duodenum. I am walking all over the hospital now. I have eaten my first meal, and I can have anything I want, even pizza and wings. I still have the feeding tube, but it is clamped off as my doctors evaluate my body's ability to digest the food I am eating. I still have the ileostomy, but this is a small price for me to pay. I am looking forward to my intestines being reconnected early next year. I am so happy because I am no longer so scared.

Katrin is still hanging in there as we're not ready for Little John to come into the world yet.

Friday, October 8, 2004

My doctor just left my room, and I am stunned at his good news. I am going to the Mologne House today, and I will be an outpatient now! Katrin has been living at the Mologne House since she came to Washington, DC. This will be my new home.

My parents are picking us up for dinner, and we are going to the Macaroni Grill. I can't wait to get in the car and go for a ride with my wife and my parents. It doesn't even matter to me that I have to take this big wheelchair with me.

Lord, before I get too caught up in my celebration, I want to say thank You again for bringing me through this ordeal. As I look back, it seems like a dream to me. You are so good, Lord. When all the prayers were coming up to You to save my life and heal my body, my progress was Your answer to all of us. We prayed unceasingly, and unceasingly You answered, "Consider it done."

SUPPORT FOR OUR HERO

by Ruth

From the moment my nephew John joined the army, our family has been bursting with pride. We are not what some people would call a "military family," but we are a patriotic family. I can still remember going to parades as a child, seeing tears roll down my dad's face as he heard the national anthem played while a color guard passed by. He loved his country, and he was proud and grateful to be an American. He appreciated the freedoms that Americans enjoy. It was not surprising that his deep patriotism was passed down to his children. We often remarked that if Dad could have seen John join the army, then without a doubt he would have been John's biggest fan.

The most loyal patriot in our family is Risë, John's mother. Even before John joined the army, she displayed patriotic decorations in her yard, home, car, and even her office. On the 4th of July, the residents that live in the assisted-living home where she works knew they would hear patriotic music ringing throughout their hallways, and they would see American flags hanging everywhere. Risë's employer always enjoyed her decorations, and even kidded her at times about the lengths she would go to in her attempts to make everyone as exuberant as she was. The true patriotism of Risë's employers would really shine when she would be paid for the many weeks she was away from her job to be with John in Germany and at Walter Reed. There aren't a lot of employers that would or could do that. Risë's employers did it without hesitation.

Risë's patriotism is contagious, and it is admirable. John's father, Bob, is a true patriot, as well. As a couple, they are the perfect parents for a soldier to have. They were so proud of John when he joined the army.

Risë and Bob are also exuberant Christians. They have raised their children in the church, and they are faithful believers. They live their lives accordingly and humbly. This is their comfort zone, and anyone who knows them knows this about them as well. Make no mistake — they love a party, playing cards, and going to the casino. I guess you could call them a well-rounded American family who enjoys life, even with all its ups and downs. They know a lot of people and are well liked. When John was injured, those friends, acquaintances, and many strangers would come forth to support them and John through their ordeal.

At the prayer vigil, we passed a notebook around for people to write messages to John and his family. "Risë and family, we are currently singing *Let There*

Be Peace on Earth. You are all in our prayers. I shed a tear tonight for your son, and he is definitely in my prayers and thoughts. I know he is a strong young man. He will make it. I look into the flame of my candle and think to myself that we all should be so thankful for what we have, and to take nothing for granted. With Love, Anthony Castanza."

"Risë, John, and family, we are keeping your candles burning at the Basilica until you return. Love, Kathie Cardamone."

"Johnny, I know you are being healed. We sang *Let There Be Peace on Earth*. You must have heard us in Germany, I am sure. Your Gram sang her best tonight!!! Your Pastor held the flag out during the song. I felt as if I was lifted off the earth giving you all my positive energy. Love, Sue Breier."

"Dear John, you're in our prayers daily and on many prayer lists around the U.S. God will take care of you. We are so proud of you for fighting for the freedom we enjoy. God Bless. Mr. and Mrs. Keith Lemke."

"John, I am here tonight to lift you up in prayer. My son just left Iraq after 14 months. God took care of him, and I pray that you have a quick and complete recovery. God bless you and your family. God Bless America! Karen Lamson."

"John and family, my nephew, Tom Tucker, is serving in Iraq. We are all connected in spirit, courage and love. God Bless. Mike Smietaner, Sr."

"Dear John, I wish you a quick return to good health and your family. A lot of people are here, and prayers are being said tonight at the vigil and for each day forward. Thank you for your courage and efforts on behalf of all Americans. May God Bless. Congresswoman Francine DelMonte."

All these people at the prayer vigil, coming together for one cause, asking God for strength and healing, was overwhelming. Is there anything more in life a person could ask for? All this was for our John. It is hard to comprehend the generosity and kindness of the American people.

The Sunday after the prayer vigil, Janet's "John Update," that had now grown to include people all over the country, John's nurses and doctors in Germany and Iraq, and his commanders and fellow soldiers in Iraq, confirmed what we had all been asking God for. "While he is still in critical condition, he is making progress every day. The most noted progress came during the time the prayer service for John was being held here in North Tonawanda on Thursday night (August 5) at 8:30. They said that John opened his eyes and became more alert and much more communicative around 9:30 p.m., our time. God is AWESOME!!! The doctors just shake their heads in amazement. He has been referred to as the Bionic Man...and also as a MIRACLE!!!"

We received email messages back from many churches, individuals, and prayer groups that were praying for John and were depending on Janet's "John Updates" so they could pray for specific needs. The long list includes St. Matthew Lutheran Church, Ransomville United Methodist Church, Fillmore Chapel United Methodist Church, Bethel Baptist Church, Eastern Hills Wesleyan, The Chapel,

Immaculate Conception, Pendleton Center Methodist Church, Forestview Church of God, St. Mary's Catholic Church of Lockport, Bergholz Rosary Group, Rev. Howie Peters of Olean, New York, The 700 Club, the Christian Broadcasting Network, The First Lightning Team in Iraq (John's fellow soldiers he served with every day), including LTC Kyle M. McClelland (John's battalion commander in Iraq), 1LT Josh Walter (John's platoon leader in Iraq), 1SG Michael Grinston from John's battery in Iraq, Christ Our Healer, 1LT Willette Balsamo, one of John's nurses at Landstuhl Regional Medical Center in Germany, SonRays Ministries, Rich Products, employees of the University at Buffalo, hundreds of friends and family, acquaintances, and even strangers.

Janet's email updates did more good than I think she realized. She had such a beautiful way of writing them, and she inspired everyone to keep praying and keep hope. She usually signed them "Love and prayers, Janet" and added her praise of God and his miracles. Everyone who received her email messages was so motivated. My nephew, Tim Joyner, is in the Navy and is stationed at Corpus Christi, Texas. In one message to Janet, he wrote, "Janet, thank you so much for all that you do!! I have started to learn more about the power of prayer. Thank you for reminding everyone to support ALL our troops; it's so important. Again, thank you."

John's cousin, Dr. Jeff Pirinelli in Dallas, Texas, emailed, "John is in our thoughts and prayers every day. His amazing recovery has been an inspiration to us and to our entire Sunday school class. Our faith has been renewed by the Lord's work through John. May God continue to strengthen and bless John and our whole family through this time of worry. Love, Jeff, Karen, and Riley Pirinelli."

1LT Balsamo emailed her thoughts to us from the hospital in Landstuhl. "Thanks again for the updates. I pray for John always and for his wonderful family. His recovery still continues to astound me. I know he may have his medical setbacks here and there, but he's still a miracle. Please keep the updates coming — I share news with other nurses and docs, and it renews our faith in what we do — and also our faith in a higher God. Keep his spirits up — he has to be destined for something great — like raising his child to be president or something!!! Who knows — only God. My love and brightest blessings, 1LT Balsamo." Most people think of doctors and nurses as being very practical when it comes to the health and progress of a patient, so for them to say they had seen a miracle was music to our ears.

"Mrs. Riggs, First, let me just say 'thank you' for your updates!!! I am John's battalion commander, LTC Kyle McClelland. I was with John during the first 12 hours of his ordeal and initial operations, holding his hand, praying for him, whispering in his ear that he will be fine. John is a special soldier...he is one of our gentle giants. I have been in downtown Schweinfurt on the weekends and often ran into him and his Cobra crew. He is a pleasure to be around. We all miss him dearly and will continue to pray for his speedy recovery.

"We have had some rough days here in Bayji, and that night was yet another setback. Take comfort in knowing that we have detained the responsible individuals, and they will be brought to Iraqi justice. I will attempt to call and speak with John and the family shortly. We have continued offensive operations to rid this area of the insurgent presence, and you can tell John that 'Cobra Strike' is doing an awesome job. We are doing great things every day here, and it is not all about death and destruction. Many, many humanitarian projects are underway, and we will continue to fight the three-block war until the day we transition with our next unit and the Iraqi Security Forces.

"Again, thank you for the updates, links and photos…I must say that John looks like a completely different person than when I last saw him!!! I talked to his initial combat medics (first responders on the scene – fellow soldiers!!!), his doctors and nurses, and they should be proud of their training and saving his life. They would all do the same for a brother in arms in the band of brothers. Wishing you and the family the best and continue to 'be strong.' The soldiers of Task Force Lightning send our warmest wishes and best regards for a healthy recovery.

"Sincerely, Kyle M. McClelland, Lieutenant Colonel, United States Army, Commander, Task Force 1-7, Bayji, Iraq."

If Janet had not put so much work and effort into the email "John Updates," we never would have received the hundreds of comforting messages back from caring friends, strangers, and family that served as fuel for John and the family.

Within days of John's injury, people were asking if there was some way they could make a monetary donation for John. Consequently, the John Pirinelli Benefit Fund was set up at a local bank. Generous and grateful Americans, many of whom were complete strangers to John, deposited thousands of dollars into that fund. This money would make a huge difference in John and Katrin's lives. Because of the stress they would experience in other ways, it was such a blessing knowing they would not have the strain of not having enough money to furnish their apartment or buy a vehicle or just have some fun. This money would serve its intended purpose very well.

The support for John from children was at the top of the list. John's nephew, James Garavaglia, James's teacher, Mrs. Crawford, and James's class of second graders from St. Matthew Lutheran School, made a Get Well Banner for John. The efforts of these youngsters were featured in the *Tonawanda News*, a local newspaper, with a picture of the kids with their smiling faces. James was so proud of his uncle, and he wanted everyone to know his uncle is a hero!

"Bookmarks to Help A Wounded Soldier." That is what the poster delivered to Cousin Janet said that displayed the bookmarks and the following message: "The second grade students at Redeemer Lutheran School in Florida have been praying for John since his injury. Their teacher, Sheryl Essenburg, was John's nursery school teacher. The kids wanted to do something to help John and decided to create bookmarks to sell to make some money for John and his family."

My heart was warmed a few weeks after John's injury when I read an editorial in a local newspaper entitled, "State Sen. George Maziarz deserves a lot of credit for this one." Mark Lindsay went on to say in his commentary, in part, "I'm as cynical as the next guy when it comes to politics. I'm even more cynical when it comes to politicians. Every now and then, though, a politician will surprise me. State Sen. George Maziarz did just that last week. By now, I think the entire world has heard the story." Mr. Lindsay went on to explain how the senator helped Philip and Stephanie get their passports. When events happen in your life that come to you through God, they will only make your life better. As the senator said, he knows he will never forget this experience, and I'm sure it has changed his life forever. What he did for John can never be understated.

A few days after the prayer vigil, I received a telephone call from Lester Robinson of Potter, Harris & Scherrer Agency, an insurance agency in Lockport, New York. Lester is the producer of the *ABC's of Insurance Complementary Health Series*. He invited me to do a segment on his series, "The Power of Prayer." Even he was convinced that John had been saved through the power of prayer, based on everything he had heard through the news media about John's injuries and his amazing recovery. He wanted me to tell his viewers about it. I was thrilled to share the good news.

On August 18, 2004, he interviewed me, and the show aired a few weeks later. I received quite a bit of feedback after people saw the show, including the following email from one of my co-workers. "Ruth, I saw you on TV the other night. You were very inspiring. Prayer is very important in my life, too."

The message had reached her, and I was thankful that God had used me to proclaim His grace. I am always happy to share John's story with anyone who will listen. I was very grateful for the opportunity Lester Robinson gave me to talk about God and the miracle of John's recovery.

"Hi, just a few cards here for your son, John. Hope he is doing better. If you get a chance to pass them on to him, we would appreciate it. They are from Niagara Mom's Play Group. Our founder, Laura, went to school with John. Also enclosed are some cards from Brownie Troop 249 from Errick Road School. Take care. D. J. Scive."

"Dear John, I am a teacher at Starpoint High School. I am a veteran of Desert Storm and have been following your story over the past few months. My heart aches for all the young men and women who are in Iraq and Afghanistan. I know how it feels to be separated from the ones that you love and not know when you're going to come home. I have been praying for you and your family. I am so glad that you are okay and will be returning home again very soon. I admire your courage and strength and wish you nothing but the best for the future. Being alive and watching your son grow up is the greatest gift of all. In honor of Veterans' Day, my English review classes wrote letters of well wishes to you and the other soldiers at the Walter Reed Medical Center. When you return to the center, would you please pass out their letters to soldiers who need them the most. Sincerely, Mrs. Kathy Broda." In that envelope were some of the sweetest and most heartfelt messages I have ever read. I know they touched the hearts of the soldiers who received them. They moved me to tears, too.

A teacher at Fricano Primary School, Ms. Kathy Cullen, had her entire second grade class make cards for John. They were so cute since her students are very young. They all had the right idea. The message was loud and clear. They all wrote, "Thank you for everything you have done for us so we can be free. We are proud of you!"

John and our family received hundreds of get well cards through the mail at Walter Reed, at Risë and Bob's home, and at my home. They were all very special in their own way and contained heart-felt messages, such as this one: "Heard about your nephew, and we are praying for his stateside return and full recovery. That boy is what makes this country great, and we so appreciate his sacrifice and courage for us, defending our freedom. My husband and I thank him again and again."

Before John reached the hospital at Landstuhl, Germany, he had already received a backpack filled with clothing, personal hygiene supplies, and spiritual support. The backpack also contained a hand-made quilt. That backpack traveled with John from the hospital in Tikrit to Germany and finally to Walter

Reed Army Medical Center in Washington, DC. Shortly after John arrived at Walter Reed, we would find out just where that backpack came from, and we would be astonished when we met the lady who actually packed it. Peggy Baker, founder of Operation First Response, came to Walter Reed to see John when we were there. The motto for this organization is "Supporting Wounded Warriors and Their Families." In our conversation with Peggy, we discovered that she had packed John's backpack herself on her dining room table right there in Virginia. There are other awesome volunteers all over the United States who prepare these backpacks as well. Some might call it a coincidence that John's backpack came from Peggy. We choose to call it a God wink.

Gail Ann Huber is a dear friend of our family and is a radio personality on Oldies 104, a local Buffalo radio station. I listen to her quite often. One morning, shortly after John was injured, I had my radio tuned in to Gail's show. I heard Gail dedicate Neil Diamond's song "America" to John. She also told her listeners about what had happened to him, how she knew him, and more importantly, she asked people to keep him in their thoughts and prayers. Several people mentioned to me later on that they heard her talking about John on the radio and how wonderful it was that she dedicated such a great song to him. We were grateful for Gail's efforts to keep the prayers going for John.

On August 10, Gail was doing the introductions for a concert at Art Park, a local theater in Lewiston, New York. She talked briefly about how she knows

John and what happened to him, and, when her remarks were finished and before the concert started, she asked once again if people would remember John in their thoughts and prayers. With her few statements, she brought an audience of over 5,000 people to their feet. The applause was deafening and overwhelming. She told us that as she looked out from the stage into the audience, she saw many, many people in tears. The support for John was phenomenal.

Another very active group of dedicated Americans, the Soldiers' Angels, contacted me and asked if I would like to come to the air show being held at the Niagara Falls Air Reserve Station on August 28 and be present at their table. This would be a great opportunity to tell people about John's injuries and ask them to pray. I jumped at the chance. Philip had come home from Washington by then, and so we went together. We had a great time talking to people about John and all our troops.

During my conversation at the air show with Mary Trudeau, a Soldier's Angel, she told me she was communicating through email to one of her soldiers, and she told him about John. To her amazement, the soldier told her he was John's best friend in Iraq and he was there when John was shot. She asked me if I had ever heard John talk about Barch. Immediately I knew exactly who she was talking about. Yes, John had told us about Barch, and we had even received photos from John of Barch and John together in Iraq.

Soldiers' Angels is a national organization. The Angels are randomly assigned to soldiers. What would the odds be that Barch would be the soldier of an Angel from the area where we live, and that we would, in fact, actually meet her? I wouldn't even attempt a guess, but I can tell you it was no accident or coincidence. It was God's plan to remind us once again that He was right with us all the time, taking care of every detail of John's life and of our lives!

I received a package in the mail from Rev. Howie Peters from the Southern Tier Military Parents Support Group in Olean, New York. Before it arrived, he called me and let me know the package was on its way. During our conversation, I told Rev. Peters I was planning to go to Washington soon to see John. He explained that the package contained a cloth he and his wife had prayed over and anointed with oil at the altar at their church. This cloth was to be placed on John's wounds when I saw him. The message with the prayer cloth said, "Greetings. Here is the prayer cloth for John. I saw on the news that he is back in the USA. Praise God. Along with the cloth is a prayer; first for strength, miracles in John's life, healing for John physically, mentally and emotionally, a quick recovery, and his return home soon. I will also pray for traveling protection and emotional strength for you. Love in Christ Always, Howie." I met Rev. Peters shortly after John was injured, but I feel like I have known him and his wife all my life. Their son, Trevor, is in the military. They can only imagine how we must feel. Their kindness was comforting, and their prayer support was uplifting and always seemed to come at the perfect time.

Our family loves country music, so when we heard the announcement around the first of July, before John was injured, that Toby Keith would be performing at Darien Lake, an outdoor theater about 50 miles from Niagara Falls, we bought tickets. We love his music, but what we also love about him is that he is a real patriot. He sings several songs about soldiers, and every one of them has become a family favorite. After John was injured, I called John Paul at 106.5 FM, WYRK, in Buffalo to see if there was some way Toby Keith could possibly dedicate a song to John at the concert. John Paul told me that wouldn't be possible, but he felt he could do something just as good. He gave me three Meet and Greet passes that would take Risë, Phil and me backstage to meet Toby Keith before the show. On September 2, 2004, we personally met, shook hands with, and had our photo taken with Toby Keith an hour before the concert began. My sister talked with Toby briefly and told him about John. He responded, "Please tell John I said thank you." To this day, the photo of Toby Keith, my sister, Phil and me is still on display in my home and probably will be for a very long time.

Toby Keith is a very talented singer and a warm and caring individual. We gave him John's army photograph and asked him to autograph it and send it to us. To tell you the truth, I doubted we would ever see that photo again. But about two weeks later, it arrived in the mail, personally signed by Toby Keith. Next to John's photo he wrote, "Thanks. Toby Keith."

During the first week of September, I received a telephone call from my cousin, Scott Mittelstaedt, who lives in Florida. Scott was very excited to tell me he and three of his closest friends were organizing a golf tournament. The John R. Pirinelli Benefit Golf Tournament would be held on Sunday, October 17, at Rocky Point in Tampa. He was wondering if anyone from the family would be able to come. Of course, Phil and I jumped at the chance. We left Buffalo on Saturday morning, October 16, and returned home on Monday. I cannot even find the words to explain how it felt to see 40+ golf carts lined up with smiling golfers in them, ready to hit the course. Each golfer was given a terry cloth towel with a yellow ribbon and "Support Our Troops" embroidered on it, and all these towels were hanging on everyone's golf bag. What a sight it was as they took off down the path to the first tee. Scott and his friends, Ed Beth, Rich Gonzalez, and Dick Blasioli, put so much work into this event. In addition to numerous donations of prizes and raffle items, they had solicited corporate sponsors for every hole.

Our cousin, Brett Herman, is a professional long-driver. Brett was at the golf tournament that day, too. For a $5 donation for John, on the fifth hole, he would hit your ball for you. I've never seen anyone hit a golf ball that far! Thanks to Brett, John bene-fited from the donations Brett collected for him that day, and I benefited because I easily parred the hole! Several friends of the organizers volunteered to man the registration table and deliver refreshments to the golfers during the tournament. After the tournament, a gathering was held at the Brewmaster Steak House in Indian Rocks Beach. We had a great time. Awards were given out, raffles were held, and we were treated to a comedy show and dinner. The mood was great because John was getting better every day. When the tournament was over and the accounting was done, the organizers and all the men and women who came to support John by volunteering their services and/or by playing golf that day raised over $5,000 for John.

Guy Gane contacted me in September. Guy owns M-One Financial Services, a financial planning business in Buffalo, and he has a keen interest in the military and supporting the troops. He urges our military personnel to take the time to make sure their financial house is in order so their families will be taken care of if they make the ultimate sacrifice. His company has a financial team of experts that U.S. military personnel can take advantage of to make sure their investments are handled properly and that their questions are answered here at home instead of worrying about them overseas. He does a radio show on Saturday mornings, and he asked me if I would like to be a guest on his show and talk about John, his injuries, and his progress.

Iney Wallens, who has a radio show in Niagara Falls that she has been doing for years, also contacted me. She invited me to be a guest on her show on October 22 to also talk about John. I had never been on the radio before, but I was starting to get used to talking to the media, so I thought, "Why not?" Both of these opportunities would be another way to get the news out about John. On October 22, I was on the Iney Wallens show, and on October 23, I was on Guy's radio show. This was another week I won't soon forget. The support for John just continued to astound us.

Pat Vergils, a co-worker and friend, called me to tell me she had something for John and that she would be delivering it to my office. Pat belongs to the Knitting Ministry, a group of women that crochets prayer shawls for people. Lovingly packaged inside a gift bag was a beautiful white shawl with soft, long fringe and stitches woven into a pattern that reminds me of gentle waves. The shawl was crocheted by Ruth Stachowiak "with a prayer woven into each stitch that you may know that you are supported by the compassionate care and concern of women living in the spirit of Saints Clare and Francis." Also enclosed was this prayer. "Dear Heavenly Father, be with John who will use this shawl. Comfort and console him as You hold him in Your loving presence. May this shawl be to him a sign of Your love and grace. May it bring him warmth when he is weary. May it surround him and cover him with love to ease pain and suffering. O Christ, be with all those who comfort those who struggle. May your strong touch reach out to heal all the broken and hurting people and places in our world. We ask Your blessing on this shawl and on John who will use it. In Jesus' Name. Amen." The prayers attached to the stitches of that shawl contributed in no small way to John's miraculous healing.

On August 14, 2004, Todd and Scott Hameister, people we have worshipped with at St. Matthew for many years, went to a NASCAR Race at Watkins Glen, New York. On August 25, Todd delivered a package to me for John with the following note enclosed: "Hello, John. We heard of your accident in church. I am praying for your speedy recovery. My son, Scott, and I went to the NASCAR Race at Watkins Glen the weekend of August 14. Scott and your cousin, Dawn, were in the confirmation class of 2000. My wife and I went to your prayer vigil at Gateway Park in North Tonawanda. I thought that you might like a signed T-shirt from Joe Nemechek. I am not sure if you are familiar with him, but he drives the car with the US Army as one of his sponsors. I gave him one of the pamphlets passed out at Gateway Park that evening with your picture on it, and the photos I have enclosed show him reading the pamphlet and signing the shirt for you. Mr. Nemechek told me that he goes to Walter Reed to visit patients, so he is familiar with your place of recovery. I will continue to pray for you and hope to see you in Western New York soon. May God send his richest blessings to you and your family. Sincerely, Todd Hameister." The T-shirt has the Army logo on it, "An Army of One," Joe's name, a picture of his car, and his autograph. It is a treasure John will have for the rest of his life.

JoAnn Abbo-Bradley, owner of Skizzors Hair Salon in Niagara Falls, wanted to show her support. On Sunday, October 31, JoAnn and her staff donated their time and talent for an entire day. All the money collected from their patrons that day was donated to John. A big yellow sign in front of JoAnn's salon read, "Cut-A-Thon to Benefit John Pirinelli." JoAnn and her staff have never met John. They said they were doing their duty as Americans.

Jim Gleeson, who owns the Laundry Lounge, a local business, was a huge supporter of John. Jim placed a gallon jar on the counter next to the cash register for his patrons to drop their change in, if they wished, to make donations to John. He gave that gallon jar full of money to John when John came home for the first time. Jim also provided financial support to John in other ways by making donations for a benefit that was held for John. He has a large sign in front of his business, and for weeks he displayed a message advertising the benefit for John.

I work for a school district in Western New York. I was at a loss for words the day the Teachers' Association Community Relations Committee announced it was sponsoring a fundraiser, and the proceeds were going to be donated to The Fisher House Foundation in honor of John. The Fisher House Foundation donates comfort homes built on the grounds of major military and VA medical centers. The homes keep family members close to injured soldiers during their hospital stays for unexpected illness or injury. Since John was injured, our family members had been staying at the Fisher House in Germany and then the Fisher House in Washington. The entrance to the Zachary and Elizabeth Fisher House in Washington displays the following state-ment next to a portrait of the Fishers: "Their gift is dedicated to our greatest national strength and trea-sure – our military service men and women and their loved ones." The cost to stay at the Fisher House is minimal. Not only is lodging provided, but also food, transportation, and a computer with Internet access. The Fisher Houses are beautiful, peaceful, and very well maintained. Many of my co-workers told me they had never heard of the Fisher House Foundation until John was injured. On January 21, 2005, a check in the amount of $1,480 was presented to the Fisher House Foundation in honor of John. Are there any words to express our gratitude? I can't think of any right now other than a simple, heart-felt "thank you."

John received a donation of four tickets to a Trans-Siberian Orchestra Concert at Shea's Performing Arts Center in Buffalo on December 1 through his cousin, Jim Pirinelli, along with a beautiful guitar signed by many of the musicians in the orchestra. John also received several tickets to a Buffalo Bills football game from Demco, a local company, and sports memorabilia signed by Buffalo Sabres and Buffalo Bills. Needless to say, these generous donations were thoroughly enjoyed by John and his family.

A few days after Bob, Risë, Philip, and Stephanie left for Germany to be with John, John's cousin, Jim, called me and asked what I thought about having a benefit for John. I thought it was a fantastic idea. Jim explained that he and his wife, Brenda, had been tossing the idea around for a couple of days that they would like to head up the organizing committee. I was thrilled with their idea. I offered my support, and shortly thereafter I received notice that the first benefit committee meeting would be held on Monday, August 23, 2004. In the meantime, we spread the word and started looking for volunteers, and before long, we had a committee of 20+

people ready, willing, and able to give their time and talents to what turned out to be a huge event with over 1,000 people in attendance. Over time, the size of the committee grew and grew.

November 5 was selected as the date for the benefit. When this date was chosen, none of us expected that John could even be there. However, with the lightning speed of his miraculous recovery, we were delighted when we found out he would be coming home the day before the benefit. What a great homecoming party this was going to be!

Soliciting donations for the benefit was not a problem. We would hardly have a chance to get the request out of our mouths, and businesses and individuals were saying "yes." Practically anything we wanted we could have. The American Legion hall, tickets, beverages, and food were all donated. Over 200 baskets were donated for a basket raffle. We received donations of a TV, barbecue grill, freezer, bicycle, stove, tools, jewelry, luggage, a getaway package, lamp, and sports memorabilia for the auction. We received donations of 50+ gift certificates to be raffled off for everything from a car wash to a haircut to a meal in a fine dining restaurant. We enjoyed the music of five live bands, and all of their time and talent was donated. Joyce Hoover, a professional videographer, taped the evening's events and donated all her time and equipment. There were 50/50 drawings every hour, and one of the highlights of the evening was when a local radio personality, John LaMond from WYRK, auctioned one of John's Grandma Klein's homemade apple pies for $100. All the local television stations and newspapers covered the event. John was a celebrity in his hometown of Wheatfield and, it seemed, in all of Western New York.

At the benefit, raffle tickets were sold for a quilt signed by Toby Keith. This quilt is very special, not just because it boasts Toby Keith's signature, but also because it is made with love. The label reads, "In honor of SPC John Pirinelli, U.S. Army, for his dedication and service to our great country. Made and donated by Kris Passinault, Hamburg, NY and Kathy McKinney, West Palm Beach, FL. Special thanks to Lena Carson, Blasdell, NY and Michele Paczka, Blasdell, NY for getting it signed by Toby Keith on 9/2/04. Completed on 10/4/04." The drawing was held on December 17, 2004, and Josh Prezioso, a friend of John's, won the quilt.

D & T Graphics from Lockport, New York, donated a huge banner. It read, "SPC John R. Pirinelli, An American Hero." We displayed it at the airport when John came home for the first time, on the front of Bob and Risë's house, and at the benefit. Every time I looked at it, I got a lump in my throat.

A lot of money was made that evening for John and Katrin's benefit. This money was going to make John and Katrin's lives a lot easier, and this made everyone extremely happy.

Right before Christmas I received a telephone call from Mrs. Fran Costa. I had never met her. She and the Giving Tree Group at Prince of Peace Church in Niagara Falls had Christmas gifts for John, Katrin, and Little John. The generosity never ceased!

Every time he was given a gift, John would remark in his humble way that he is not a hero. No matter how we tried to convince John he might have done something extraordinary in his life, he always deferred to those men and women who have died and made the ultimate sacrifice defending freedom. In our prayers, we have asked God if, some day in some way, He would help John realize he is a special person and that he has done something very few people do. In my heart, I felt God's answer. "I have told you in the Bible, through my son, Jesus Christ, that humbleness is good and it is honorable. John will understand he is a hero. I will choose the right time to make it happen. You can consider it done."

COMING HOME

by John

I have "come home" so many times. When you're in the military, coming home is the highlight of your life. I have had a few different "homes" in the last year, and each homecoming has been special to me.

After I was shot on July 28, 2004 and left Iraq, my homecoming was to Landstuhl Regional Medical Center in Germany after two days at FOB Speicher in Tikrit, Iraq. Landstuhl was my home for a week, and I don't remember much of the time I spent there.

My next homecoming was on August 9, 2004 when I arrived on American soil at Walter Reed Army Medical Center in Washington, D.C. My memories of that homecoming are very dim. Obviously, it was not my first choice for how and when I should come home early, but I was happy to be there.

October 8, 2004 was the next homecoming for me. That was the day I left Walter Reed AMC and went to my new home at the Mologne House, a huge and very nice hotel-like building next to the hospital. There Katrin and I set up "housekeeping." The Mologne House is very attractively decorated and well maintained. Our room had two double beds, a TV, a small refrigerator and microwave oven, a table and chairs, and two dressers for our clothing. We also had our own bathroom. We set up a small nursery in one corner of the room for Little John who would be coming soon. I was so thankful Katrin had been able to continue to carry him until now. In fact, when we went to the Mologne House, I was glad we would have a few more weeks to once again adjust to a new way of life.

The one thing I brought from the hospital to my new home that was going to be difficult for me was the ileostomy. When I was fully dressed, you couldn't even tell it was there. No matter how hard I tried, I simply could not get used to it. In fact, I hated it. I felt so self-conscious in front of my wife. I could tell it didn't bother her. She would have changed it for me if I asked her to, but there was no chance of me ever doing that. Once in a while it would burst, and that was a terrible mess to clean up. Katrin was so good about it. Even though I didn't want her to, she would jump right in there and clean it up with me. The doctors told me it was only temporary, and I hoped and prayed they were right. I shouldn't have complained. There are so many wounded soldiers so much worse off than I was. I saw them every day.

During Katrin's visit with my family in New York in July, when she met my family for the first time, they had a baby shower for her. When my mother came back to Washington for the birth of Little John, she brought many of those gifts to us. A volunteer group at Walter Reed AMC also had a baby shower for us. Little John had plenty of everything and anything a new baby might need. We were so blessed to have so many people caring for us in so many ways.

During the next few weeks, I continued to go to the hospital every day for physical therapy and doctors' appointments. Little by little I gained my strength back. I was still very thin. I had lost almost 60 pounds since I was injured. I looked totally different. Katrin was feeling pretty good, too, even though the last few weeks of her pregnancy seemed to drag. When I was still in the hospital, we were worried that Little John would come early, but now we were anxious, and anytime would be good.

Little John was born at the National Naval Medical Center in Bethesda, Maryland by cesarean section on October 25, 2004. He was healthy and beautiful, and Katrin came through the surgery successfully. We were both ecstatic we had cleared this hurdle. I felt better than I had felt for a very long time, mentally, physically, and emotionally. Now all the attention was on Little John, and that's just the way I wanted it. He weighed eight pounds, six ounces, and he was 20 inches long. Mom took some digital photos to email to my Aunt Ruth. I didn't have to wonder what Aunt Ruth was going to do with those photos. We were seen on the evening news at home that night.

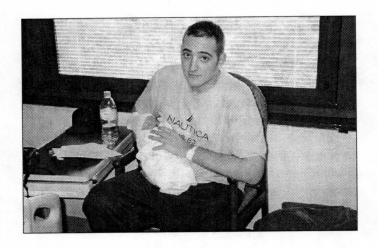

On this day I held my son in my arms for the first time. He is the person who gave me the strength and determination I needed to fight for my life.

Katrin and the baby spent the next four days in the hospital. I stayed there with them. Soon it was time to come home to the Mologne House. Now our one-room home was filled with the sounds of our baby's quiet breathing and newborn cries. Both sounds were music to my ears.

Here we are at home at the Mologne House.

We spent the next week getting used to being parents. I had to go the hospital every day to do my physical therapy and see my doctors. I was feeling pretty good, but I was still very tired. Katrin decided she wasn't up to going to Niagara Falls with me on the upcoming Thursday for the benefit/homecoming.

While not the most important "homecoming" for me since my injury, Thursday, November 4, 2004, was one of the most exciting. I was going to see all my friends and family, and they were so excited to see me. They repeatedly called me their hero. I repeatedly told them I wasn't a hero. The heroes have come home in flag-draped coffins as far as I was concerned.

I knew there were going to be TV reporters at the airport when I got off the plane in Buffalo with my dad. My aunt had already warned me so I could get mentally ready for it. Apprehension was written all over my face. I had received so much media attention during the last 14 weeks. Some people would enjoy all that attention, but being in the limelight is not my comfort zone.

As I rounded the corner at the gate and walked toward the main terminal, there stood at least 30 friends and family, some who had taken off work to be there, waving their American flags, cheering and clapping their hands. My two cousins, Mike and Jeff, were holding an eight-foot banner that read, "SPC John Pirinelli, An American Hero." There were balloons in the air, and the little children in the family were running toward me with flags in their hands. The reporters were there with their cameramen. And, lo and behold, who would be standing there clapping and cheering right along with everyone but Senator Maziarz.

The senator just happened to be on a flight from Albany that had arrived a few minutes prior to mine. When my Aunt Ruth saw him walking down the corridor, they looked at each other in amazement. She told him why we were there, so he stayed and welcomed me with everyone else. With all the senator had done for my family because of me, he had never met me. Does that sound like a coincidence to you? It doesn't to me. Mom, Dad, Phil, and Steph hadn't seen the senator since he helped Phil and Steph get to Germany when I was injured, so it was like a reunion for all of them, too. Senator Maziarz was getting married the following weekend, and his stag party was the following day. He still found time to come to the benefit for me. The senator has always found time for me and for my family. What is so incredible is we didn't even know him before all of this happened.

I talked with the reporters for a few minutes, they took some pictures, and then it was time to go home. I was so happy to have that over with. It is stressful, and I wanted to make sure I said the right thing.

I was very anxious to get back to my parents' house and visit with everyone. I still had the feeding tube but it was still clamped off, so I could eat almost anything I wanted. Pizza and wings from my favorite pizzeria were waiting for me. A beer tasted pretty good, too.

Friday, November 5, was a very big day for me. I went out in the morning, did some errands, and visited with friends and family. I noticed as I was driving down the street to my parents' home that for a couple miles there were yellow ribbons tied around the trees and telephone poles. I thought it looked really nice, and asked my dad how long they had been there.

"Since the day before yesterday, John. They were put there for your homecoming." I was speechless.

I was nervous about all the attention I was going to get at the benefit. The organizers told me they thought there might be 1,000 people attending. I could not imagine what this evening was going to be like. I wished I could share all this attention with some of my army buddies who I believed deserved it more than I did, but they were still in Iraq fighting the war.

The benefit started at 4:00 p.m., but I decided I wouldn't go there until 7:30. I was still pretty anxious when I got around a lot of people, and I knew it was going to be crowded. I was still having problems with crowds and feelings of claustrophobia.

When it was finally time for me to go to the benefit, my brother Rob picked me up, and we entered the building through a side door. I don't think I've ever seen so many people in one room in my life. Toby Keith's song, "American Soldier," was playing very loudly, and when the people saw me, they just started clapping. A lot of them were crying, and I was, too. I just could not believe all of this was for me.

My brother, Rob, his wife, Tracey, and even their daughter, Little Gabby, supported me with heart and soul.

I brought a bouquet of flowers and an angel necklace for my mother. The band on stage at the time asked my mother to come to the front of the hall where I was standing. When she got there, I gave her a big hug and the flowers, and my Cousin Risë put the necklace on her. Mom was so happy to see me, and I was happy she was standing next to me. She always gives me strength when I need it.

A program had been planned, and my parents and I were asked to come up on the stage. The program started with the Young Marines presenting the colors. We all said the Pledge of Allegiance and sang the national anthem. I was marveling at these young people in their camouflage uniforms, all poised and serious about their duties as loyal Americans. I wondered how many would become soldiers some day. I silently prayed they would never have to fight in a war.

Two government officials were there with proclamations, one from the Town of Wheatfield where I grew up and one from the County of Niagara. They both declared November 5 as John Pirinelli Day. In his November 2004 newsletter, Supervisor Timothy Demler said, "On November 5, Wheatfield and our community honored SPC John Pirinelli for his service in our military and being critically injured under enemy fire in Iraq. As a special honor to a special friend, the Town of Wheatfield honored him by proclaiming November 5 as John Pirinelli Day in Wheatfield."

Legislator William Ross read the Niagara County proclamation and was also very gracious in his remarks.

In my mind, there are people living in the Town of Wheatfield and the County of Niagara who have made huge sacrifices and have done greater things than I have done. I sure hope a day or two have been named after them, but I kind of doubt it.

Then, to my complete surprise, Philip, with his incredible voice, accompanied by my cousin Jim Pirinelli, sang a song they wrote just for me, "My Brother, My Hero." I wanted to burst out crying during the song, but I tried to hold back my tears until the end.

(Phil sings):
We grew up side by side, and we were pretty tight.
Thanks to Mom and Dad, they taught us
what was right.
And through the years, I've watched you grow.
And here we are now, and I want you to know,
You are my hero, oh, you are my hero.
As we grew up we saw some loved ones die,
But I always knew I'd have you right
there by my side.
Life ain't always easy, and sometimes pretty rough.
You were always with me if things got too tough.
You are my hero, oh, you are my hero.
And with you lying there, my eyes fill up with tears.
You are a warrior; you have a lot more years.
You did your job so well that the Army had you do.
Your family, friends and country are
so proud of you.
Now the next stage of your life has just begun.
You are home now, Stitch, with your family,
wife, and son.
You are my hero, oh, you are my hero.

We are all together now, right where we should be.
God has blessed my life so much by
keeping you with me.
Now it's time for me to go, I've got some
things to do.
I am so proud you're in my life. You know
that I love you.
You are my hero, oh, you are my hero.
And with you standing here my eyes fill
up with tears.
I think of all the fun we'll have through
the coming years.
(Phil speaks):
John, first of all, I'd like to say, I'm glad you're
home, man. It's been a long couple months. You've
got more healing to do, but the bottom line is you're
home and you're safe, and you're my hero and
you're our hero. You did your job. You did what was
asked of you. You sacrificed yourself and your body.
I just want you to know that you're my hero.
(Phil sings):
You are my hero, oh, you are my hero.
You are my hero, oh, you are my hero.
You are my hero, oh, you are my hero.

***When Phil was singing, I once again experienced
the depth of his brotherly love.***

When the song was over, I walked over to Phil on
the stage, put my head on his shoulder and cried.

My cousin Kristy said it all when she said a few
days earlier, "For most people, the kindest things
said about them are spoken at their funeral. John is
very lucky. He is finding out how much people love
him when he is still alive."

Even with all the wonderful tributes I had just
experienced, I still wasn't feeling well. I just wanted
to get out of the center of attention, so I decided to
have a seat next to my grandmother. It was a lot
easier being next to her. I sat down, and it wasn't
long before my nerves calmed down.

I have always felt so close to my Grandma Klein.
She was another source of strength for me
when I needed it.

After an hour, it was time for me to go. I couldn't do it anymore. I was so thankful no one was holding that against me. They just wanted me to be happy. They kept telling me I had been through enough. Everyone was so kind to me, and I really appreciated it. I worried I might not be showing it, though. I left and went home where it was quiet. I contemplated all that had just happened.

The next day a reporter from The Buffalo News came to my parents' home to interview me. The article in the paper that day read, in part, "Army SPC John Pirinelli doesn't believe for one minute that he's a hero. And his family is just happy to have him home from Iraq in one piece. Pirinelli, 23, who was critically injured July 28 in an ambush near Tikrit, is back in his native Bergholz. He arrived Thursday night and spent Friday surrounded by family and friends in the house where he grew up. The family carport was filled with balloons and welcome home signs. Friday night, he got a taste of just how many folks from his hometown have been pulling for him...' I appreciate it,' said Pirinelli...'but it's like so many people are out there getting hurt that don't get this. Why do I deserve this more than anybody else?'" I wanted to be sure people knew there were thousands of soldiers out there who needed their support. I hoped I was able to get that message across.

So far, all my homecomings were unforgettable.

Sunday came, and it was time for me to go back to Washington to be with Katrin and Little John. I didn't want to be gone too long, but they were doing well, and I was very happy about that. I got back that night, and Katrin and I relaxed with our son. The next day we began making plans to return to my hometown. I was still active military, and I was going to bring them home and go back and forth to Washington, as necessary, until I was discharged. My tour of duty was supposed to end on July 10, 2005, but I seriously doubted that was going to happen.

Friends of my Aunt Ruth, Carol and Joe Wawrzynski, offered to rent their home in the Town of Niagara to us as they were living in Florida for the winter. Their home was completely furnished and so comfortable. Carol and Joe's generosity made our move from Washington to my hometown so easy. This arrangement also gave us time to settle in and figure out where we wanted to live. Katrin and I both needed recovery time. Once again, a complete stranger "came to our rescue." We made our move home to Niagara Falls in November, just in time for Thanksgiving.

Thanksgiving is one of our favorite family holidays. Our pastor at St. Matthew leads an extraordinary church service year after year. Baskets of food are collected for those less fortunate, and the service is centered on giving thanks for God, country, and all the blessings we have received. Needless to say, this was going to be a very special day for me and for my family. We also wanted to somehow convey our thanks to all the hundreds of people who had shown such compassion and generosity to me and to my family. My parents placed the following ad in all the local newspapers:

Thank you!

Because of the prayers and support of so many people, Army SPC John Pirinelli will spend the holiday season at home with his friends and family. "Thank you" to everyone that has contributed in any way since John was wounded in action in Iraq on July 28, 2004. Your good deeds are very deeply appreciated.

With gratitude and warmest wishes for a peaceful holiday season,
SPC John Pirinelli and Family

We then prayed that each and every person who had supported me would somehow see our message and know it was meant just for them.

We lived at Carol and Joe's until we rented our own apartment in March 2005. Even though we appreciated the use of their home, it was good to get our own home with our own furnishings. My leaves were becoming shorter and shorter, and I would have to spend more time in Washington. I didn't have a job in the army, and when I went back, I would see my doctors and continue to work on my rehabilitation and discharge.

Katrin became more self-sufficient each time I left home to return to Washington. It was good for her, too. With all the stress we had suffered, we were grateful our lives were beginning to quiet down a bit.

On February 9, 2005, the doctors reconnected my intestines and removed the ileostomy. The surgery went well and I was elated, to say the least, when my body confirmed a few days later that all its functions were back to normal. My duodenum had healed, and this was another miracle for me.

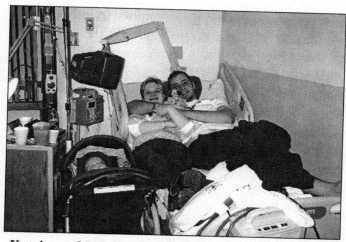

Katrin and I were thankful that one more surgery was behind us. We hoped we were getting close to the day I could say I was completely recovered.

Good news came once again in April when I received word that the 1st Infantry Division was returning from Iraq and the army was going to bring me to Germany to celebrate with my fellow soldiers. I was elated and couldn't wait to go.

When I arrived at the airport in Frankfurt, Germany, I was not ready for the reception I received. I felt like I was the President of the United States. I was greeted with open arms and received a hero's welcome.

On May 6, 2005, Major General John R. S. Batiste delivered a speech in front of a crowd of 4,500 soldiers and their families and friends, as well as the families of soldiers in our division who had died in Iraq. I will never forget the words he spoke to me and four other soldiers who had been wounded in Iraq. "I would also like to recognize some special soldiers, all wounded in action, who returned to be with their comrades during this important day. Private Robinson, Specialist Covington, and Specialist Pirinelli of 1st Battalion, 7th Field Artillery; Sergeant Laurent of 1st Squadron, 4th Cavalry; and Staff Sergeant Andrews of the 9th Engineer Battalion; it is great to see you here today, and we all wish you a speedy recovery. Your sacrifices have not gone unnoticed, and you will be forever part of the 1st Infantry Division. Thank you for your courage and all you have given. Please join me in a round of applause for these incredible warriors."

The weeklong celebration was just what I needed. I enjoyed seeing my army buddies again, and thankfully, everyone who was in my unit when I left Iraq came back to Germany in one piece.

A notable moment occurred when I came face to face with Colonel Russell Dragon. I saluted him, and he said to me, "No, John, I salute you," and then he hugged me and saluted me. So he thought I was a hero, too. Although I felt very honored, I prefer to continue to give all the credit to those soldiers who have lost their lives.

I had a great time in Germany, and it was not easy to say goodbye to my buddies. I was thinking of Katrin and Little John at home waiting for me, so that thought made it easier for me to leave Germany. I had another great homecoming the day I saw Katrin and Little John again.

The Wheatfield Democratic Club contacted me before I went to Germany for the reunion. This organization wanted to dedicate an evening to myself and another local soldier, Sergeant Jonathan Joyce, because we were their "hometown heroes." On May 10, 2004, Sergeant Joyce was credited with eliminating an insurgent who was about to fire an RPG from an ambush position on a U.S. patrol outside Baghdad, thus saving the lives of five U.S. soldiers and a vehicle. He also engaged 30 other insurgents in a ten-minute firefight, which allowed his unit to move out of the combat zone. He was awarded the Army Commendation Medal, with valor. He is a hero in my eyes and in the eyes of many others.

After my visit to Germany, it was becoming a little bit easier for me to deal with all the attention I was getting, and on Saturday, May 21, 2005, my family and I attended the Wheatfield Democratic Club's "Home of the Brave" dinner dance when Sergeant Joyce and I were honored. I was very proud to stand next to Jonathan that night. It was a very nice evening, and I felt good.

I was proud to have my photo taken with Jonathan Joyce and New York State Assemblywoman Francine DelMonte at the "Home of the Brave" dinner dance.

Shortly after that event was Memorial Day. I was asked to ride in a parade in the City of Niagara Falls. Jonathan Joyce and I rode together, and I took Little John with me in our vehicle. A bandstand had been set up at the end of the parade route where a special ceremony would be held. Once again, Jonathan Joyce and I received awards and commendations from various government officials and military organizations. It was a beautiful, sunny day, and I really appreciated the kindness of everyone there.

Before long it was July 28, 2005, and it was the first anniversary of my injury. Cousin Janet took a photo of Little John, Katrin and me and sent it with the following email to all the people on her email list whom she had kept informed about my condition during the time I was in the hospital.

Here we are on the first anniversary of my injury.

"Can you believe it was a year ago today that John was shot in Iraq?? God certainly has been good and answered our many prayers...and then some!!!

"John is doing very well and is still waiting for his medical release from the army. He has to go to Washington periodically as he is still considered as being stationed at Walter Reed Hospital. John, Katrin, and Little John live in a condo in Niagara Falls. They are still waiting for 'life after the army' and some sense of normalcy. Little John keeps them busy, and he is a welcome focus for keeping life in perspective.

"Looking back on the events of the past year brings so many thoughts and memories – more good than bad – some horrific and many beyond wonderful!! The power of God has been the strength and life-line through it all. John and the whole family are so grateful for your part in praying for John's miracle(s!) and for being the wind beneath their wings. Life's priorities certainly shift when you see how precious life is and how quickly it can be snatched away. You realize how meaningless things are and how precious people are. You are precious!!!

"We all have much to be thankful for and God is to be praised!!"

No one can say it like Janet does. She has been so devoted to me, my family, and everyone who has supported us through our ordeal. She never got tired of spreading good news.

Janet made sure she forwarded to me the following response to her anniversary email from Willette Balsamo, 1LT, Army Nurse Corps, one of my dedicated nurses at Landstuhl:

"Dear Janet, You won't believe this – this morning I was going over all my emails from you during the past year, and I was thinking of you all SO strongly, then I opened my mail this afternoon and there you are!!! Wow!!! I was absolutely thrilled. It's so wonderful to see the pictures of John, Katrin, and Little John. I got teary eyed remembering how he looked at Landstuhl and how Katrin stood by his bed endlessly, so hugely pregnant and so very, very worried and scared. The wedding pictures on the wall...Risë's face when she first came into the room...everything, like it was yesterday instead of a year. You just don't know how much it means to a nurse to see such a miracle as John is – he's destined for a great and higher good – that's why he survived, not just from modern medicine, but divine intervention as well, and most of all, love.

"I'm leaving for Tikrit, Iraq to work in the ICU there in September. I'll be there a year. As I take care of wounded soldiers, I'll be thinking often of John when I hear those words, '20% chance of survival'... and I'll remember John and his entire family. The patient will then become personal for me, and I'll be fighting like hell (pardon me) for that other 80%.

"My love to all of you and brightest blessings to that beautiful little family of John, Katrin, and that gorgeous Little John."

This is Willette displaying a blanket my mother sent to her for Christmas. The words on the blanket say it all. "Nurses are all heart. God's special Angel Willette."

During the next year, I continued to travel between Niagara Falls and Washington as I worked through the medical boards and paperwork involved with my discharge. On January 28, 2006, I had my eleventh and what I hope will be my final surgery at Walter Reed. The huge hernia I had in my abdomen was repaired. I was surprised to find out that Dr. Andrew Friedman would be assisting with this surgery. Dr. Friedman was the doctor in Iraq who took care of me immediately after I was injured. Once again, I was able to see that this was no accident or coincidence that Dr. Friedman was at Walter Reed to perform this final surgery. God had placed him there, and what a blessing this was to me.

Dr. Friedman and I spent quite a bit of time talking about the events of the night of July 28, 2004 when I was shot. This humble man told me things about that night I had never heard before, including the fact that it was actually the skill and wisdom of Dr. P. J. Schenarts that saved my life. While Dr. Friedman did the initial surgery, hours later Dr. Friedman and Dr. Schenarts performed another surgery and Dr. Schenarts knew exactly what procedure to use to begin the repair of the extensive damage done to my intestines. This conclusion to the medical portion of my journey was perfect.

After a few months of healing, I was notified that I was going to be retired from the army. I was also notified that I would be promoted and would retire as a sergeant. Once again, this was very good news for me and my family. A retirement from the army will be a tremendous asset to me for the rest of my life, and I am very grateful.

Before I was injured, I considered staying in the army, but I believe now that God has a different plan for my life. My final homecoming and retirement was on April 9, 2006. Not only is April 9 my wife's birthday, but more importantly, April 9 is the day three of my fellow soldiers were killed during the mayor's office situation in Iraq that I was at as well. When these brave men died, I knew I would never forget that day. How incredulous it is to me that God would choose that sacred day as the day I would retire from the army. Once again God reminded me that He is in control of every detail of my life.

God saved my life. It is a miracle, and it is plain to see, not just to me, but to hundreds of people who watched God working so hard in my life and in the lives of all those around me. My plan now is to tell people about what God has done for me. "I will spread the word, Lord. I have seen Your power, love, and amazing grace. I will tell all who will listen to me how You have blessed me. You can consider it done."

A QUILT FULL OF LOVE

☆ ☆ ☆

Within a few hours after John was injured, he received a backpack filled with personal hygiene items, clothing, prayers, and inspirational support from Operation First Response, a group of dedicated volunteers in the States who assemble these backpacks for our wounded soldiers. John's backpack and its contents traveled with him from Iraq to Germany to Washington, DC.

Also included inside the backpack was a hand-made quilt. As John moved from hospital to hospital, many of his doctors and nurses wrote the following messages on the quilt.

"No more stopping bullets with your guts. See you in Garrison. LTC Clagett."

"Our thoughts and prayers are with you. Get well soon. Lt. McClendon."

"John, you are a true fighter! Keep up the progress! Good luck in the future. CPT McLaughlin."

"If you can, keep your head when all about you are losing theirs. Good work. Thank you. Godspeed. CPT Kent."

"We picked up the ball after the 67th CSH sent you on the way. The Landstuhl team in the ICU went out 200% to get you where you are today. I hope that you continue to make great improvements. You have a great family to help you along. All our best. Dr. Warren Dorlac."

Dr. Dorlac spent endless hours with John at Landstuhl, diagnosing his injuries and formulating his treatments.

"Scars are sexy! LT Mona Bullard."

"I was one of your nurses. You were great. Good luck with the new baby! (Enjoy.) Take care of yourself. Michelle Hardin."

"The best of luck to you. Continue to keep your positive attitude as you continue to fully recover. Remember, the key to a good marriage is communication and compromise. The key to being a good patient is patience. Continue to drive on. Lt. Haley."

"Good luck. You're doing great. Get well soon. Dr. Andrew Shorr."

"It's been a while since I saw you in Tikrit. I have had the distinct privilege of taking care of you twice. It's an honor to serve those like you who have given so much. Dr. Andrew Friedman."

During a visit to Walter Reed AMC in March 2006, John, his nephew, James, and James' traveling pal "Flat Stanley" visited Dr. Friedman to thank him once again for all he had done for John.

"It's been an honor to get to know you over the past few months. Thank you for your service and sacrifice in defense of our country. You've been through a great deal, but your positive attitude, strong, supportive family, and I'm sure a few thousand prayers have seen you through and will continue to do so. Congratulations on the pending birth of your child. Enjoy your con leave. We'll meet again soon for round #? I've lost count! Dr. George Peoples."

"You really gave us a run for our money!! We worked very hard to get you home. Make the most of the life ahead of you. Dr. P. J. Schenarts."

(Written next to Dr. Schenarts' words was a message from Dr. Friedman. "This is the guy who saved your life.")

The precious messages on this quilt will be preserved and treasured for generations to come. Someday, if John's grandchildren ask him why he has so many scars on his belly, this quilt will help him tell the story of how, with the help of God, "an army" of dedicated people worked so hard to save his life.

THE AUTHORS

☆ ☆ ☆

Risë, John, and Ruth at Niagara Falls, New York

**For the Pirinellis, the power of Niagara Falls is
like the power of God.
It is awesome, you can depend on it, and, for the
moments you are there,
it takes you to a place like none other.**

The Pirinellis feel blessed that God chose them to
live through this experience.

Even though it was very scary at times when it
seemed that John would not
survive, the blessings received by watching God at
work were abundant.
It is their hope that this book will touch
the lives of many
who, after reading it, will forever after believe.

To them, that will be yet another miracle.

☆ ☆ ☆

Korean War Veterans Memorial
Washington, D.C.
March 25, 2006

☆ ☆ ☆

"I am very proud of my country,
and I wouldn't change a thing."

SGT John R. Pirinelli, Retired